Elon Musk and Tesla

Other titles in the *Technology Titans* series include:

Jeff Bezos and Amazon

Larry Page, Sergey Brin, and Google

Mark Zuckerberg and Facebook

Reed Hastings and Netflix

Steve Jobs and Apple

Technology TITANS

Elon Musk and Tesla

Stuart A. Kallen

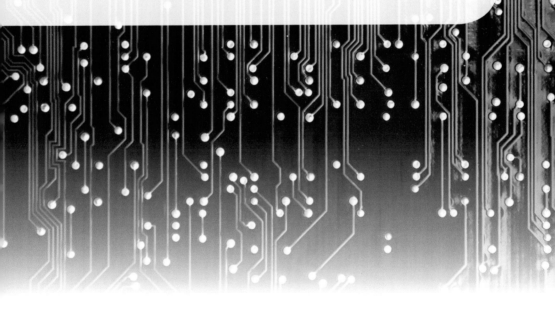

ReferencePoint Press®

San Diego, CA

LIBRARY OF CONGRESS CATALOGING-IN-PUBLICATION DATA

Kallen, Stuart A., 1955- author.
  Elon Musk and Tesla / by Stuart A. Kallen.
     pages cm. -- (Technology titans)
  Audience: Grades 9 to 12
  Includes bibliographical references and index.
  ISBN-13: 978-1-60152-870-4 (hardback)
  ISBN-10: 1-60152-870-1 (hardback)
1. Musk, Elon--Juvenile literature. 2. Tesla Motors--Juvenile literature. 3. SpaceX (Firm)--Juvenile literature. 4. PayPal (Firm)--Juvenile literature. 5. Businesspeople--United States--Biography--Juvenile literature. 6. Businesspeople--South Africa--Biography--Juvenile literature. 7. Clean energy industries--Juvenile literature. I. Title.
  HD9710.U54M87 2016
  338.7'6292293092--dc23
  [B]
                                                    2015003560

Contents

Introduction   6
Solving Problems for Humanity

Chapter One   9
The Wonder Years

Chapter Two   22
PayPal Payoff

Chapter Three   36
Launching SpaceX

Chapter Four   51
Tesla Motors

Source Notes   65

Important Events in the Life of Elon Musk   70

For Further Research   73

Index   75

Picture Credits   79

About the Author   80

Solving Problems for Humanity

Those who follow the tech industry know that Google founders Larry Page and Sergey Brin changed the way people use search engines on the web. Amazon.com founder Jeff Bezos changed the way the world shops online. Apple founder Steve Jobs transformed communications with the introduction of the iPhone. And all these farsighted individuals made billions of dollars. But the soft-spoken Elon Musk, the genius behind the electric car company Tesla Motors, has dreams far bigger than creating the next generation smartphone or e-commerce website. Musk wants to redirect the destiny of the human race. As he said in 2013, "For me it [is] never about money, but solving problems for the future of humanity."[1]

Musk's plans for the twenty-first century involve changing the way people travel on Earth and the way they fly through outer space. With the Tesla automobile, powered by seven thousand battery cells linked to electric motors, Musk wants to move humanity beyond polluting gas-powered vehicles. With the rocket ships he builds at his company SpaceX, Musk wants to colonize Mars.

> "For me it [is] never about money, but solving problems for the future of humanity."[1]
>
> —Elon Musk.

From the Freeway to Mars

As an engineer, designer, and CEO of several companies, Musk is not afraid of high-profile—and high-risk—ventures. With the Tesla Model S, he redesigned the basic automobile and built an electric car with speed, elegance, and performance beyond almost any other vehicle on the market. And along with beating gas-powered Porsches and Ferraris at the racetrack, the futuristic Tesla is easy on the environment. When charged with solar cells, the Tesla produces zero carbon dioxide (CO_2), the greenhouse gas responsible for climate change.

Musk's plans for the future go far beyond the freeway. In 2002 he founded Space Exploration Technologies, or SpaceX. The company develops and manufactures rockets and spacecraft that resupply astronauts at the International Space Station. Like Tesla, SpaceX is a risky venture. Until Musk founded the company, the only entities to successfully launch a spacecraft were the United States, China, Japan, India, Russia, and the European Space Agency. But SpaceX is about more than money. As Musk explained to reporter Ross Anderson in 2014: "I think there is a strong

Elon Musk displays an automobile manufactured by Tesla Motors at a 2009 press conference.

humanitarian argument for making life multi-planetary in order to safe-guard the existence of humanity in the event that something catastrophic [like extreme climate change] were to happen . . . because humanity would be extinct."[2]

Back from the Future

Musk can afford to dream big: In 1999 he became a multimillionaire at the age of twenty-seven when he sold his web software company Zip2 for $300 million. He used his profit of $22 million to create PayPal, an online financial service that was acquired by eBay for $1.5 billion in 2002. Musk earned $165 million from the deal, which he plowed into Tesla Motors and SpaceX. In 2015, at the age of forty-four, Musk was worth an estimated $12 billion.

> "Elon has already gone to the future and come back to tell us what he's found."[3]
>
> —Tosca Musk, Elon Musk's sister.

Elon's sister, Tosca Musk, once joked, "Elon has already gone to the future and come back to tell us what he's found."[3] And Musk's future contains more than fast cars and rocket ships. Musk is a visionary who wants to slow global warming, grow food on Mars in greenhouses, and help humanity become a true spacefaring civilization.

Chapter 1

The Wonder Years

Like one of his sleek electric Tesla automobiles, Elon Musk's heritage is complicated. He was born Elon Reeve Musk on June 28, 1971, in Pretoria, South Africa. His mother, Maye Musk, was a dietitian and fashion model from Canada, but she was raised in Pretoria. His father, Errol Musk, was an engineer and businessman of English descent born in South Africa. After Errol and Maye married, they had three children in three years. Elon is the oldest, and he was followed by a brother, Kimbal, and a sister, Tosca.

Elon (pronounced *ee*-lon) has said that people think his first name is from some exotic location. However, Elon got his name from his great-grandfather, John Elon Haldeman, who was sheriff of St. Paul, Minnesota, around 1900. Elon's grandfather, Joshua Haldeman, was the family adventurer. He moved with Maye and the rest of the family from Canada to Africa in the 1950s. With a strong interest in archeology, Haldeman flew all over southern Africa in a small Cessna airplane searching for the ruins of the ancient lost city of Kalahari. He never found the mysterious archeological site. Later he made another lengthy trek by racing in and winning a road rally from South Africa to Cairo, Egypt. He made the journey in the family station wagon. Haldeman was also the first person to fly from South Africa to Australia in a single-engine plane. Haldeman's spirit of adventure runs in the family, according to Tosca Musk: "Without sounding patronizing, it does seem that our family is different from other people. We risk more."[4]

Different from Other Children

According to his mother, Musk was an extremely quiet, shy child. When he was very young she thought he might be deaf. Elon could hear just fine, but even as a young child he was far different from other children. Elon read continually, not just for enjoyment but to advance his knowledge. And his studies could be put to practical use, according to the following story that is part of Musk family lore.

When Elon was six, he was playing outdoors in the summertime with his siblings. As the sun set the other children headed for home, begging Elon to follow. Elon refused to go inside because he thought the dark night was beautiful. Tosca, then three years old, began to yell and cry, blurting out that she was afraid of the dark. Maye finally came out to see what was going on and found Elon euphoric with a beaming smile. According to Maye, Elon raised his arms in the air and yelled out: "Do not be scared of the darkness! There is nothing to fear—it is merely the absence of light!"[5]

Elon's genius made him stand out when he started school in Pretoria—but not in a good way. He was the youngest and smallest kid in his school and also the target of bullies. According to Kimbal: "It's pretty rough in South Africa. It's a rough culture. Imagine rough—well, it's rougher than that. Kids gave Elon a very hard time, and it had a huge impact on his life because there was no recourse. In South Africa, if you're getting bullied, you still have to go to school. You just have to get up in the morning and go. He hated it so much."[6] Due to this "rough" treatment Musk considered himself an outsider even at an early age. And when he was around nine, his life was further upended when his parents divorced. But Errol Musk remained in his children's lives. The Musks shared joint custody of Elon and his siblings, who spent weekdays with their dad and weekends with their mom.

Rockets and Chocolate Bars

Errol was a businessman involved in numerous enterprises. With Elon by his side, Errol often flew his small airplane north to Zambia where he had an interest in an emerald mine. Zambian customs officials were notoriously corrupt, and Errol would carry sacks of chocolate bars to bribe them. As Kimbal recalls, "You basically would give them chocolate

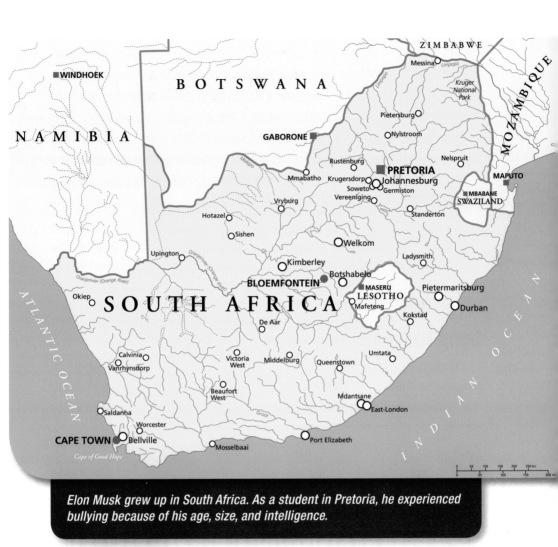

Elon Musk grew up in South Africa. As a student in Pretoria, he experienced bullying because of his age, size, and intelligence.

bars, and they'd allow you to do business."[7] Watching his father, Elon picked up negotiating skills that would serve him well in later years.

Musk also learned from his father to try new things even if they might be dangerous. For example, Elon loved spaceships, so Errol encouraged him to make homemade rockets and explosives. As Musk recalls, "It is remarkable how many things you can explode. I'm lucky I have all my fingers."[8]

Creating a Video Game

When Elon was ten years old he spotted a computer at a Johannesburg electronics store. Although his father could not see any practical purpose for the primitive computer, Elon persuaded him to pay for half of the three-hundred-dollar machine. Elon saved up his allowance for the other half. The computer was a Commodore Vic20, which contained less memory than a modern coffee machine. However, the computer represented endless possibilities to Musk. He spent countless hours teaching himself to write computer code. Musk recalled his feelings about the computer years later. "I was like, 'Whoa, I mean, you can actually write games and programs?' It seemed like the most amazing thing."[9] In 1983 Musk designed a video space game called *Blastar*, inspired by his love of spaceships. He sold *Blastar* for $500, which was more than he paid for the computer.

> "I'm nauseatingly pro-American. . . . The U.S. is where great things are possible."[12]
>
> —Elon Musk.

Deep Thoughts

In addition to his other interests, Musk was a voracious reader when he was in his teens. He sometimes consumed two books in a single day. In addition to technical books, he read about religion and philosophy. One of his favorite books was the best-selling science fiction novel *The Hitchhiker's Guide to the Galaxy*, written in 1979 by Douglas Adams. The humorous story follows a character named Arthur Dent who travels to the ends of the universe. Throughout the story Dent is searching for what the book describes as "The Answer to the Ultimate Question of Life, the Universe, and Everything."[10] The answer, delivered at the end of the book by a massive computer called Deep Thought, is a meaningless number—"42." Although Adams said he chose the number as a simple joke, the answer spawned thousands of discussions on Internet chat forums. The answer also resonated with Musk who later said:

> It taught me that the tough thing is figuring out what questions to ask, but that once you do that, the rest is really easy. . . . I came to the conclusion that we should aspire to increase the scope and scale of human consciousness in order to better understand what questions to ask. Really, the only thing that makes sense is to strive for greater collective enlightenment [by asking the right questions].[11]

South African Dissatisfaction

When Musk was seventeen he decided that his path to personal enlightenment required him to become a United States citizen. Musk later described his motivation: "I'm nauseatingly pro-American. I would have [moved there] from any country. The U.S. is where great things are possible."[12]

Musk had other reasons to move. At the time, South Africa was an international pariah, shunned by other nations and multinational corporations. This was due to South Africa's long-standing racial policy, known as apartheid; about 15 percent of the nation's white population brutally repressed the black majority.

Although the apartheid system was collapsing in the late 1980s when Musk yearned to be an American, South Africa was still gripped by racial violence and repression. The apartheid government relied on a military draft to maintain power, and every eighteen-year-old South African male was required to serve. Musk wanted nothing to do with South Africa's

South African soldiers march in a parade. Musk's reluctance to serve in South Africa's military led him to emigrate from that country to Canada.

compulsory military service: "I don't have an issue with serving in the military per se, but serving in the South African army suppressing black people just didn't seem like a really good way to spend time."[13]

Becoming Canadian

Because of the apartheid situation, it was difficult for South Africans to obtain US citizenship. However, Musk found it was easier for Canadians to become American citizens. Musk's mother was originally from Canada, which allowed him to obtain a Canadian passport. Against his parents' wishes Musk bought a plane ticket to Montreal, where he arrived in 1988 nearly broke.

Musk spent the following year knocking on the doors of his Canadian relatives, unannounced, seeking room and board. He would find a job, stay a few weeks or months, and move on. Many of his relatives lived in rural areas where Musk found minimum-wage jobs. He worked weeding vegetable patches, shoveling grain, and cleaning out boilers at a lumber mill while wearing a hazmat suit.

In 1989 Musk enrolled in Queen's University in Kingston, Ontario. However, his economic struggles continued; attending school while working part-time, Musk was living on about one dollar a day after paying rent and college expenses.

Despite the hardships, Musk refused to return home. As Maye Musk states, "Elon went to visit my family and he never came back."[14] In fact, Musk was able to convince the rest of his family that life was better in Canada. One by one they followed him to Ontario; the fifteen-year-old Tosca was first, followed by Maye, then Kimbal. Soon all his cousins on his mother's side made the move across the Atlantic. Only Errol stayed behind in Pretoria.

The Musks settled in a small Toronto apartment where Elon slept on a pullout sofa. But in 1992 the Musks moved again, this time to the United States after Elon was accepted to study business and physics at the Wharton School of the University of Pennsylvania.

Visionary Projects

At Wharton, Musk managed to earn money while amusing himself. Musk and his roommate, Adeo Ressi, rented a fourteen-room house and staged huge parties. They charged a five-dollar entrance fee, and sometimes there were more than five hundred people in attendance. Musk managed the finances while Ressi, an artist, gave the interior of the house a club-like appearance. Ressi filled the rooms with sculptures, art installations, and paintings decorated with Day-Glo, a type of paint that shines luminously under a black light.

One of Ressi's sculptures was a wooden desk, tipped over on its side and painted with fluorescent colors. The ever practical Musk managed to convert the wild art piece into useful furniture; he righted the desk and set up his computer on top. Ressi picks up the story: "I'm like, 'Dude, that's like installation art in our party house.' It wasn't a desk. It was a work of art. The argument about this went on and on." When asked about this in 2012, Musk says, "It was a desk."[15]

In addition to throwing parties to pay the rent, Musk wrote visionary business plans. In 1995, about a decade before Google began scanning millions of books and making them available online, Musk envisioned an electronic book-scanning company. Musk also drew up plans to produce a type of energy storage device called an ultra-capacitor or supercapacitor. This device can accept and deliver an electrical charge much faster than rechargeable batteries. The futuristic capacitors, still in the experimental phase in 2015, will likely be used someday in electric cars and other vehicles.

Three Important Problems

In 1994 Musk received a bachelor's degree (BA) in economics from Wharton. He decided to stay another year to obtain a BA in physics. Although Musk's plans for the future were uncertain, he knew he wanted to delve into what he called three "important problems." According to Musk, "One was the Internet, one was clean energy and one was space."[16]

These subjects led Musk to Palo Alto, California, where he was accepted into the high energy physics program at Stanford University in 1995. Palo Alto is located in the middle of the high-tech region called Silicon Valley, and much of the research that led to the modern Internet was conducted at or around Stanford.

In 1995, Musk became a student at Stanford University (pictured), but dropped out after only two days to pursue a career involving the fledgling Internet.

In 1995 the World Wide Web (as it is known today) was only a few years old. Although the public was just learning about the Internet, the concept was generating a great deal of attention among scientists, researchers, and business leaders in Silicon Valley. Musk realized he did not need a graduate degree to tackle the first of his "important problems," the Internet. He dropped out of Stanford after only two days with the idea of starting an online company. Musk commented on the Internet craze of the time: "I could either watch it happen, or be part of it."[17]

Founding Zip2

Musk became part of the Internet craze when he founded Zip2 Corporation with Kimbal. The company developed software that would allow news organizations to publish maps, city guides, and business directories online. When Musk conceived Zip2, there were few companies that specialized in converting print content from traditional newspapers and magazines into electronic media. According to Musk, "We decided that finding a way to help them root their media to the internet would be a sure way to generate revenue. There was no advertising revenue on the internet at the time. . . . I started Zip2 by writing a program that allowed you to keep maps and directions on the Internet and a tool that allowed you to [change and update the] content; kind of a really advanced blogging system."[18]

While Musk was unsure if Zip2 would be successful, he thought it was worth the risk, as he stated in 2009:

> You know, worst-case scenario if the business failed, I could just go to graduate studies. [That would have been] a pretty soft landing if things didn't work out. And I thought they probably wouldn't actually. If you had asked me, I would say the odds were likely that I would probably not succeed and, therefore, I would be back [at school]. But I thought I may as well give it a try.[19]

Musk and Kimbal founded Zip2 with around $4,000 in seed money. The company, with a single computer, was located in a tiny office in Palo Alto that rented for around $400 a month. Rather than move into an apartment, the Musk brothers bought couches that converted into beds. They wrote computer code during the day, showered at a nearby YMCA, and slept in the office at night. Musk felt that pinching pennies, what he called a low money "burn-rate," was the only way to get the company off the ground: "When you are first starting out you really need to make your burn-rate ridiculously tiny. Don't spend more than you are sure you have."[20]

The Zip2 Idea

Elon Musk and his brother, Kimbal, started Zip2 with a few thousand dollars in 1995. After four years in business the Musks sold the company for $300 million, the largest cash transaction for an Internet company at that time. Musk describes the idea behind Zip2:

> With Zip2, the idea was just to try to do something useful on the Internet that other companies would find useful and would pay us at least enough to keep the doors open. So we started off with maps and directions and Yellow Pages [a telephone directory of businesses]. We branched that into publishing and interfacing with [various older] databases, particularly [those] that were of use to the newspaper industry. [The] newspaper industry was mostly not online in '95 and was trying to get online. And they had these old mainframes [large computers] that had all the data and were very difficult [for newer computers] to talk to. So what Zip2 essentially did was this model [that] evolved into helping newspapers . . . create compelling web sites. So we had customers and investors—*The New York Times*, [and media companies] Knight Ridder and Hearst.

Quoted in Knowledge@Wharton, "Entrepreneur Elon Musk: Why It's Important to Pinch Pennies on the Road to Riches," May 27, 2009. http://knowledge.wharton.upenn.edu.

"Quite Valuable in the End"

After a few months Zip2 was successful enough to attract investors. And the company grew quickly after Musk made deals to provide local maps, news, entertainment listings, business addresses, and related online content to major media outlets such as the *New York Times* and *Chicago Tribune*.

Within a few years the company that Musk had cofounded with a few thousand dollars was worth millions. In February 1999 the computer corporation Compaq bought Zip2 for $300 million cash. At the time, this was the largest cash amount ever paid for an Internet company. Ever humble, Musk commented on the Zip2 sale: "I didn't really expect to make any money. If I could make enough to cover the rent and buy some food that would be fine. As it turns out, it turned out to be quite valuable in the end."[21] Valuable indeed; after the money was split among him, Kimbal Musk, and other investors, Elon walked away with $22 million. He was twenty-eight years old.

Marriage and Family

While Musk was running a valuable startup, he made time for courtship. He had met Justine Wilson while attending Queen's University; the couple had dated for a time, and they had gone their separate ways. In 1999 Wilson was an aspiring novelist working as a bartender in Canada, when Musk called her from Silicon Valley. She began flying to Palo Alto for short visits, and Musk proposed marriage soon after selling Zip2. As Wilson tells the story:

> "When you are first starting out you really need to make your [money] burn-rate ridiculously tiny. Don't spend more than you are sure you have."[20]
>
> —Elon Musk.

> Although I'd been dating a struggling 20-something entrepreneur, I was now engaged to a wealthy one. Elon had sold Zip2 . . . and was worth about $22 million overnight. He bought and renovated an 1,800-square-foot condo: We now had a place of our own. He also bought a million-dollar sports car—a McLaren F1—and a small plane. Our day-to-day routine remained the same (except for the addition of flying lessons), and Elon's wealth seemed abstract and unreal, a string of zeros that existed in some strange space of its own.[22]

The Musks soon moved to Los Angeles where they had a baby boy, Nevada Alexander. However, tragedy occurred when the ten-week-old infant was napping. Nevada was struck by Sudden Infant Death Syndrome (SIDS). This term describes the unexplained death of a seemingly healthy baby less than a year old, usually during sleep. The Musks were determined to have more children, and Justine gave birth to twins, and later triplets, all within a period of five years. She also found time to write three novels published by Penguin and Simon & Schuster.

Right Place, Right Time

There is little doubt that Elon Musk was highly intelligent and had a talent for business. But he also seemed to have a knack for doing the right thing in the right place at the right time. He started Zip2 at the beginning of what would be called the dot-com bubble. At the time, investors were showing intense interest in any company involved with the World Wide Web.

Breathing Rarified Air

When Justine Wilson was dating Elon Musk in 1998, Musk's company Zip2 was a struggling startup. By the time the couple married in 2000, Musk was worth over $22 million. Justine Musk describes life in the early years of her marriage, meeting actors, rock stars, and billionaires while living in Los Angeles:

> We were breathing rarefied air. The first crowded apartment we'd shared in Mountain View [California] seemed like ancient history from our 6,000-square-foot house in the Bel Air hills [of Los Angeles]. . . . We had a domestic staff of five; during the day our home transformed into a workplace. We went to black-tie fundraisers and got the best tables at elite Hollywood nightclubs, with Paris Hilton and Leonardo DiCaprio partying next to us. When Google cofounder Larry Page got married on [Virgin Group CEO] Richard Branson's private Caribbean island, we were there, hanging out in a villa with [actor] John Cusack and watching [U2 lead singer] Bono pose with swarms of adoring women outside the reception tent. When we traveled, we drove onto the airfield up to Elon's private jet, where a private flight attendant handed us champagne.

Justine Musk, "I Was a Starter Wife: Inside America's Messiest Divorce," *Marie Claire*, September 10, 2010. www.marieclaire.com.

By the time Musk sold Zip2 to Compaq in 1999, the stock values of Internet-based companies like Amazon, eBay, America Online, and others had soared into the billions. However, in early 2000, soon after Musk collected his $22 million payoff, the dot-com bubble burst. While some companies such as Amazon and eBay survived, dozens of formerly significant Internet companies filed for bankruptcy. It is doubtful that Musk could have sold Zip2 for such a huge sum had he waited a year. And soon after the purchase, Compaq was struggling financially; the company eventually merged with Hewlett-Packard in 2002.

For Musk, the periodic rise and fall of the stock market held little interest. Having solved the Internet portion of his three "important problems" with Zip2, he had his eye on the other two goals, converting the world to clean energy and conquering space. But Musk needed more money to pursue his big ideas. At least he no longer had to sleep in his office.

> "Elon's wealth seemed abstract and unreal, a string of zeros that existed in some strange space of its own."[22]
>
> —Justine Musk, Elon's first wife.

Chapter 2

PayPal Payoff

Elon Musk is a man who is not afraid to take risks. With little funding he dropped out of college to start the Internet company Zip2. And when he made $22 million in profit from the sale of Zip2, he immediately plunged $10 million into a new venture. In 1999 Musk founded X.com, an online banking and money transfer company.

Unlike Zip2, which Musk founded at a time when few were investing in the Internet, X.com entered a crowded field. In the late 1990s numerous companies were providing ways for customers to transfer funds by e-mail. They included Western Union's BidPay and Citibank's c2it. These companies made money by charging a fee of around 5 percent on each transaction; if a person transferred one hundred dollars, the online bank charged five dollars. Musk had a different concept; X.com would offer a much lower transaction fee. However, making a profit with a low transaction fee was a problem that Musk had not yet solved.

Consumer-to-Consumer

Musk was inspired to create X.com after observing the growing popularity of the eBay website. When it was founded in 1995 by computer programmer Pierre Omidyar, eBay was one of the original consumer-to-consumer (C2C) websites. On C2C sites, private sellers put up items for sale for purchase by other consumers. In the case of eBay, items are sold at auction to the highest bidder. By charging between twenty-five cents and two dollars to sellers for posting their auction notice and by taking a small percentage of the sale, eBay made money simply by providing a place for buyers and sellers to meet.

The popularity of eBay grew substantially during the early years of the dot-com boom. By 1997 the site had around half a million users conducting over 2 million sales per year. Consumers were selling thousands of products to other consumers, including books, clothes, video equipment, and computers. However, most eBay sellers were private individuals; they did not accept credit cards for payment. Instead eBay relied on old-fashioned payment methods; buyers wrote checks or bought money orders and mailed them to sellers using the US Postal Service. This system significantly slowed the buying and selling action on eBay.

Launching PayPal

Some of the most technically advanced eBay users relied on Palm Pilots to bid on items for sale on the site. Palm Pilots were early handheld computers categorized as personal digital assistants, or PDAs. Although PDAs are

In the early years of the auction website eBay, many technologically savvy buyers bid on items using Palm Pilots (early handheld computers, shown here). The software application PayPal enabled them to pay for their purchases electronically as well.

primitive compared to modern smartphones, in the late 1990s they were seen as miraculous. Users could connect PDAs to their personal computers, send and receive e-mail, set appointments, shop, and monitor eBay auctions. By 1998 there were about 4 million PDAs in use in the United States.

It was obvious to thirty-two-year-old former stock trader Peter Thiel that eBay needed a way to transfer funds electronically between consumers. According to Thiel, PDAs would solve eBay's payment problems: "All these devices will become one day just like your wallet. Every one of your friends will become like a virtual, miniature ATM."[23] To achieve this goal, Thiel cofounded a company called Confinity in Palo Alto in December 1998 with twenty-four-year-old computer scientist Max Levchin.

In September 1999 Confinity launched a new software application called PayPal to move funds from one Palm Pilot to another. An article in *Wired* magazine explains how PayPal works: "Sending a payment involves entering the amount into the Palm and transferring it to another with the 'beam' function. The device figures out who the recipient and sender are, and the next time the sender logs on to PayPal's site the payment is processed."[24] In order to attract new customers, PayPal started a rewards program. The company offered ten dollars in the account of all new users who provided an e-mail address and credit card number.

"All these [personal digital assistants] will become one day just like your wallet. Every one of your friends will become like a virtual, miniature ATM."[24]

—Peter Thiel, cofounder of Confinity.

New Rules for Financial Services

Several months before PayPal's launch, in March 1999 Musk formally incorporated X.com. In Musk's words, the goal of X.com was "to combine all consumers' financial services needs into one Web site, such as banking, brokerage, and insurance."[25] Unlike many others in the late twentieth century, Musk did not view money as pieces of paper currency but as small bits of digital information represented by numbers on a computer monitor. As he told students in a speech at Stanford in 2012:

[When] you think about it, money is low bandwidth. You don't need some sort of big [Internet] infrastructure improvement to do things with it. It's really just an entry in the database. Since the paper form of money is really only a small percentage of all the money that's out there, why not innovate financial services on the Internet? So, we thought of a couple of different things we could do. . . . [We] had a little feature that took us about a day. It was about emailing money from one customer to another. Basically, you could type in an email address . . . and transfer funds or conceivably stocks or mutual funds from one account holder to another.[26]

PayPal's Peter Thiel

Peter Thiel does not have as high a public profile as his PayPal cofounder Elon Musk. But Thiel, who was worth $2.2 billion in 2014, is one of the most successful entrepreneurs in Silicon Valley. He was an early investor in Facebook when few envisioned the possibilities of social media. Thiel also founded investment and venture capital firms worth billions of dollars.

Thiel was born in 1967 in Frankfurt, Germany. His middle-class parents moved to the United States when he was an infant, eventually settling in Foster City, near San Francisco. Like Musk, Thiel was an avid fan of science fiction and computer games while growing up. As a teen he excelled at chess; Thiel was a chess master, rated as one of the highest ranked players under twenty-one years old in America. He was also obsessed with the fantasy trilogy *Lord of the Rings* by J.R.R. Tolkien. After he made $55 million from the sale of PayPal in 2002, he founded several companies named after Tolkien references including a data company called Palantir, which takes its name from the "seeing stones" in *The Lord of the Rings*.

While Musk used his PayPal profits to build rockets and electric cars, Thiel became one of the most successful technology investors in the world. In 2015 he was investing in companies working to extend human longevity by designing tiny computers the size of molecules that could be introduced into the body to repair cancer cells. Thiel, who expects to live to be 120, sees death not as an inevitable end but as a problem to be solved.

With his unique ideas Musk was able to attract top talent to X.com, hiring Bill Harris to act as company president. Harris was the former CEO of Intuit Corporation, makers of accounting software including Quicken and the best-selling tax-preparation software Turbo-

> "Money is low bandwidth. You don't need some sort of big [Internet] infrastructure improvement to do things with it. It's really just an entry in the database."[26]
>
> —Elon Musk.

Tax. Harris boasted to the *Wall Street Journal* that he had received offers from more than one hundred tech startups. He chose X.com because he saw it as "a blank canvas upon which to write new rules on the delivery of financial services."[27]

Musk also enticed top-rated investors to back X.com. The company received $25 million in startup funds from Sequoia Capital, a venture capital firm that provides financing for high-potential startup firms in exchange for a percentage of company ownership.

In December 1999 X.com went "live." Musk put the site online with the promise to place all of the user's financial services in one place. Musk also made an offer that eclipsed PayPal's program: Anyone who opened an online checking account with X.com would receive a $20 gift card that could be used for cash at any ATM. In addition, anyone referring a friend would receive another $10 cash card. Within two months the generous offer attracted over one hundred thousand customers.

Musk Buys PayPal

Even as Musk worked tirelessly to move X.com toward success, he had his eye on PayPal. By this time PayPal had abandoned its PDA efforts, choosing instead to focus on online auction transactions. PayPal's designers created a logo with a link that connected eBay auctions with PayPal services. With this move PayPal's number of registered users doubled to one hundred thousand within weeks. However, the company's euphoria over the figure did not last long. According to PayPal vice president of marketing Eric M. Jackson:

> X.com, watching every change on our Web site, followed us onto eBay within a matter of days. Our competitor soon launched its own version of [a link and] logo for auction sellers. . . . X.com also

In March 2000, Musk (at right, pictured with Confinity cofounder Peter Thiel) acquired the online financial transaction service PayPal.

revamped the content on its homepage, toning down the "all your financial services in one place" messaging in favor of descriptions touting its ability to conduct auction payments.[28]

Jackson was unaware at the time that Musk would soon be his boss. X.com and Confinity began discussing a possible merger in December 1999; Musk and Thiel wanted to join forces to create a single online bank that would overshadow all other financial services on the Internet.

Viral Growth

In March 2000 X.com bought Confinity. Under Musk's direction PayPal set up a unique way to generate income. Anyone who sold an item on eBay would pay a small fee on every transaction; buyers paid nothing. The sale fee was around 30 cents plus a 1.9 to 2.9 percent surcharge on the purchase price. (The percentage depended on the type of formula that was used for the transaction; commercial sellers paid more than individuals.) That meant that if an individual sold an old computer for $100, PayPal would collect $1.90 (1.9 percent) plus a 30-cent sale fee, for a total of $2.20.

Musk dropped the names X.com and Confinity, and in 2001 the company's name was officially changed to PayPal. By this time PayPal was experiencing remarkable growth due to its association with eBay. This was due to what Musk credits as his viral marketing strategy. Viral marketing refers to marketing techniques that use social networks to produce massive increases in brand awareness. As customers spread the word to others, the process replicates itself like a virus. As Musk describes it, "[Customers] act like a sales person for you by bringing in other customers. In PayPal's case, they would send money to a friend and, essentially, recruit that friend into the network, so we had this exponential [increasingly rapid] growth. The more customers, the faster it grew. It was like bacteria in a Petri dish; it just keeps going."[29]

> "In PayPal's case . . . the more customers, the faster it grew. It was like bacteria in a Petri dish; it just keeps going."[29]
>
> —Elon Musk.

Unlike almost every other major corporation PayPal did not have a sales force or a vice president of sales. The company did not even spend money on advertising. Through viral growth alone PayPal multiplied its customer base from 100,000 to over 1 million in 2000.

New Competition

As PayPal grew, numerous other companies decided to start their own online banking sites. Foremost among them was eBay itself, which partnered with the bank Wells Fargo to purchase an online payment service called Billpoint in early 2000. However, Billpoint charged a hefty 4.75 percent transaction fee on eBay, and few customers were willing to use the service. Another online banking entrant was the Internet portal Yahoo!, which launched an e-commerce effort called PayDirect. The financial giant Bank One created eMoneyMail which charged one dollar per transaction.

Working at PayPal

In the late 1990s Internet tech companies were changing more than the way people conducted business. They were also transforming the way people worked in an office, as Eric M. Jackson quickly discovered. Jackson had previously been employed by what he calls the "buttoned-down" accounting firm Arthur Andersen. Here he describes his first day at work in September 1999 as PayPal's vice president of marketing:

> The interior didn't look at all like Andersen's staid high-rise arrangement of staff consultants' nondescript cubicles sitting opposite their managers' glass encased offices. Heck, it didn't even resemble the dot-com work environments with vaulted ceilings and postmodern furniture shown in television commercials. Instead it felt more like a dorm. Board games, especially "Risk," littered the floors. Engineers collected old Domino's pizza boxes on their desks. Employees wore shorts and T-shirts to work, convenient attire when the occasional water gun fight broke out in the hallways. A ratty couch with sagging cushions sat next to the entrance of [computer scientist] Max Levchin's office, which he shared with two other coders. Could anything but chaos come out of such a setting? I had plenty of time during the afternoon to mull over that question as I sat largely ignored behind my mammoth desk.

Eric M. Jackson, *The PayPal Wars*. Los Angeles: World Ahead, 2004, p. 56.

Smaller firms were also hoping to profit from e-commerce services. A small startup called gMoney gained attention by donating 220 bicycles to the University of California at Berkeley for students to share. While Musk and Thiel had once planned to dominate Internet banking, PayPal suddenly had many competitors. As Jackson writes: "In the course of just a few weeks, a sector that did not exist six months earlier had become crowded. . . . PayPal's road to 'world domination' was suddenly well traveled, indeed."[30]

eBay also created problems for PayPal. The online auction company changed its policy to eliminate the large logos placed in its pages by e-commerce sites. The move was aimed directly at PayPal, and it forced the company to shrink its link on eBay pages by 75 percent, to the size of half a stick of chewing gum. With the rule in effect, buyers found it more difficult to use PayPal.

Raising $100 Million

In addition to eBay's changing the logo rules, PayPal had other problems. While Musk preferred to have a low monetary "burn-rate," PayPal was burning through millions of dollars. Transactions were free to buyers, while $90,000 in signup bonuses was being paid every day of the week. In the three months since the X.com-Confinity merger, the company brought in only $1.2 million while spending $23 million.

Despite PayPal's money woes, Musk and Thiel were able to take advantage of the dot-com boom to raise funds for the company. And at the time, according to the stock market called NASDAQ, technology companies were booming. NASDAQ tracks the stock prices of over three thousand companies, many in the technology sector. Investors follow what is called the NASDAQ index, which is based on the value of the market's stocks. When the NASDAQ index number goes up, it means investors believe technology stocks are a good deal. They buy the stock, which drives up prices and pushes the NASDAQ index higher. When the NASDAQ index goes down, investors are selling tech stocks because they believe their value is falling.

On March 10, 2000, the NASDAQ index reached an all-time high of 5,039. With tech investors feeling optimistic, Thiel was able to travel the globe and raise $100 million from wealthy financiers, enough to keep PayPal afloat for at least a year. A few weeks after the $100 million was safely in the bank, the NASDAQ index began to fall as the dot-com bubble burst. Within a year the index stood at around 2,500, about half its previous value. At this point it would have been impossible to raise the needed funds for PayPal. According to Jackson, "The stock market's collapse would have taken [PayPal] with it. . . . It's unlikely [Thiel] could have secured such a large infusion of funds."[31]

Growing Pains

With the large cash infusion, PayPal continued to grow even as the NAS-DAQ index plunged. Meanwhile, people continued to buy and sell on eBay while finding their way to PayPal's smaller logo. But as new customers were drawn to PayPal, the company experienced growing pains in the way it dealt with customer service.

In 2000 PayPal was receiving thousands of e-mails every day from people who had experienced errors on the website or had problems with their bank accounts. The number of unanswered e-mails soared to one hundred thousand, causing great frustration for some PayPal users. If customers tried to call the PayPal phone number, they might be put on hold for more than thirty minutes. And when aggravated sellers tried to close their PayPal accounts they had to wait up to three weeks for their checks to arrive in the mail.

The customers experiencing PayPal problems filled online message boards with angry rants. This development was as big a threat as any others that PayPal had faced. The same mechanisms that drove viral growth could lead to viral collapse if the number of angry customers grew rapidly. Musk realized that the only way to solve the problem was to quickly increase the size of the PayPal customer service department. However, this would be impossible to do in Silicon Valley. At the time, the unemployment rate in the region was 1 percent, and salaries were high. Few people were willing to take jobs dealing with customer phone calls and e-mails.

Musk came up with a solution to stem the flow of exasperated customers. Within a month PayPal set up a new customer service call center in Omaha, Nebraska, where five hundred people were hired on the spot to answer phones and solve account problems. Additionally, several company employees began monitoring and responding to queries on community message boards like AuctionWatch and Online Traders Web Alliance, used by PayPal customers with problems. According to Jackson, these strategies offered solutions:

> Having employees answer questions on third party message boards did not turn around the customer service nightmare overnight, but

it did lay the groundwork for a communications strategy that would prove critical in the coming months. And with our Omaha center . . . opening its doors, this gave us an outlet to reassure our customers that better times lay ahead.[32]

Keeping Long Hours

Musk worked hard to solve PayPal's problems. He kept long hours, attended most meetings, and paid attention to even the smallest details of day-to-day management. As Jackson explains, "As I got to know him I realized Elon was nothing like the brash [millionaire] the press made him out to be. . . . Elon worked incredibly hard and cared a tremendous deal about his company."[33]

Musk needed to work hard; by October 2000 PayPal was losing $150,000 a day. Part of the problem was blamed on fraud. As PayPal became a household name, Internet-savvy criminals across the globe were devising high-tech methods to convert stolen credit cards into cash on the company's website. In one case, an organized crime ring in Russia used computers to randomly create hundreds of fraudulent accounts. This cost PayPal $5.7 million over a four-month period. By the end of 2000 PayPal was losing $2,300 an hour to hackers, cheats, and criminals.

Defeating Hackers

With problems continuing to fester, PayPal's board of directors asked Musk to step down from his role as CEO. Musk remained on the board of directors. Thiel took over as PayPal CEO and enlisted company cofounder Max Levchin to bring fraud problems under control.

One mechanism invented by Levchin addressed the fact that sophisticated criminals were using a computer program to create dozens of bogus accounts at a time. Once the accounts were created they could be used to siphon money from PayPal through various means.

Levchin needed a way to complicate the creation of PayPal accounts without causing problems for legitimate users. The solution is commonly seen today on thousands of websites. Levchin devised a box with a series of random letters that are slightly distorted and appear on a yellow background crisscrossed with thin black lines. The human eye can easily pick out the string of letters but a computer cannot. To open a new account users simply type the letters into a box on the PayPal website.

Selling Shares of Stock

With its fraud problems under control, PayPal's viral growth continued. At the beginning of 2001 around half of all payments on eBay were handled by PayPal. The company had 5 million accounts, and it was processing $1 billion annually. By this time Musk, Thiel, and other executives were making plans to sell stock in PayPal to the general public. This process is called an initial public offering, or IPO.

With an IPO, a company offers millions of stock shares on the New York Stock Exchange (NYSE) for a certain price. If investors believe the company will be profitable, the price can climb on the first day the shares are offered. In such cases the company offering the IPO can collect billions of dollars in a single day. And unlike money borrowed from banks, money earned from selling stocks does not have to repaid, even if the share price declines.

The IPO process is extremely complex, takes at least four months, and involves numerous lawyers, bankers, and accountants. While PayPal's team was working on the IPO, the most devastating terrorist attack in United States history occurred. On the morning of September 11, 2001, terrorists hijacked fully loaded passenger jets. They flew two planes into the World Trade Center in New York City and one into the Pentagon, headquarters of the US military in Washington, DC. The terrorist attack killed nearly three thousand people. When the twin towers of the World Trade Center crumbled in the middle of New York's financial district, the American economy plunged into recession.

"Elon was nothing like the brash [millionaire] the press made him out to be. . . . Elon worked incredibly hard and cared a tremendous deal about his company."[33]

—Eric M. Jackson, PayPal vice president of marketing.

PayPal executives, including Musk, were criticized for going forward with an initial public offering (IPO) of stock so soon after the devastating September 11, 2001, terrorist attack on New York City's World Trade Center (pictured) in the heart of the financial district.

PayPal Goes Public

On September 28, 2001, little more than two weeks after the terrorist attack, PayPal announced it was moving forward with its IPO. The company was widely criticized in the press for the timing of the move; the ruins of the World Trade Center were still smoldering in downtown Manhattan. In addition, the company, which had never turned a profit, seemed on track to lose nearly a quarter-billion dollars in the coming year. Financial analysts predicted PayPal's IPO would fail when investors refused to buy the stock.

Despite the dire predictions, PayPal's IPO was successful. On February 15, 2002, the company offered 5.4 million shares of itself at thirteen dollars a share. The stock price quickly rose to over twenty-one dollars a share. After expenses paid to law firms, bankers, and accountants, PayPal generated around $70 million for operating expenses. At the office, PayPal employees were blaring music and dancing on their desks. Thiel ordered kegs of beer and snacks and organized an afternoon party in the parking lot.

Purchased by eBay

The value of PayPal's stock moved up and down in the following months. But one PayPal competitor, eBay, realized it had lost the battle for e-commerce supremacy. In July 2002, rather than continue to fight a losing battle with its Billpoint payment system, eBay purchased PayPal for $1.5 billion. The thirty-one-year-old Musk, who owned 11.7 percent of PayPal stock, walked away with an estimated $180 million. He had owned the company for little more than two years.

By 2015 PayPal was one of the largest online financial businesses in the world. The company had over 100 million active accounts in 190 countries. PayPal was used on the websites of the world's largest corporations, including Wal-Mart, Netflix, and Starbucks. What had once been Musk's dream of e-commerce "world domination" was now a modern reality.

Chapter 3

Launching SpaceX

After eBay bought PayPal in 2002, the thirty-one-year-old Elon Musk was wealthy beyond his dreams. With the $180 million he received he could have retired, traveled the world, sponsored numerous charities, or even built a mansion on a private tropical island. But Musk was still interested in the "important problems" he imagined in 1994 when he graduated from Wharton—the Internet, clean energy, and space. Musk had already conquered the Internet with Zip2 and PayPal, and his clean energy plans were still in the future. Motivated by his childhood fascination with launching rockets, Musk decided to pursue space exploration by founding the Space Exploration Technologies Corporation, or SpaceX.

A Great Photograph

When asked why he created SpaceX Musk tells a story. He describes how he stayed up late one night in 2001 searching NASA's website for information about possible future missions to Mars. Musk was interested in such missions because he had conceived of a project called the Mars Oasis. He wanted to send a small greenhouse to Mars with seeds planted in a nutritious gel. The seeds would sprout into living plants, temporarily establishing life on the Martian surface. As Musk later described it: "You'd wind up with this great photograph of green plants and red background—the first life on Mars, as far as we know, and the farthest that life's ever traveled. It would be a great . . . shot, plus you'd get a lot of engineering data about what it takes to maintain a little greenhouse and keep plants alive on Mars."[34]

Musk started to price out the Mars Oasis and discovered that building a space capsule for his Martian greenhouse was relatively inexpensive. However, he would have to rely on NASA to take the greenhouse to Mars. And this dream was quickly deflated when he realized NASA had no plans for missions to Mars. Musk describes his reaction: "At first I thought, jeez, maybe I'm just looking in the wrong place! Why was there no plan, no schedule? There was nothing. It seemed crazy."[35]

Founding SpaceX

As someone who refused to take no for an answer, Musk decided to buy his own rocket to launch a space capsule carrying the Mars Oasis. However, the least expensive American rocket cost around $130 million. Since that was more than two-thirds of his PayPal money, Musk sought a cheaper way to carry out his goal. He traveled to Russia several times in 2001 and 2002 attempting to buy old Soviet intercontinental ballistic

Musk's vision for the Mars Oasis included greenhouses similar to the structure pictured at the center of this artist's rendering.

missiles (ICBMs), which had once carried nuclear bombs. The Russian missiles would have cost $10 to $20 million, but Musk could not finalize a deal.

On his last flight home from Russia in 2002, Musk realized that he would have to build his own rockets if he wanted to send life to Mars. In the weeks that followed he hired about a dozen space engineers. With $100 million of his own money he founded SpaceX in Hawthorn, California. Musk described his motivations in 2003: "I like to be involved in things that change the world. The Internet did, and space will probably be more responsible for changing the world than anything else. If humanity can expand beyond the Earth, obviously that's where the future is. Besides, rockets are cool. There's no getting around that."[36]

> "If humanity can expand beyond the Earth, obviously that's where the future is. Besides, rockets are cool. There's no getting around that."[36]
>
> —Elon Musk.

Competing with Powerful Countries

When Musk founded SpaceX, the idea that a startup company could build rockets and launch space missions seemed implausible. Rocket science, technically called astronautical engineering, is extremely complicated and costly. At the time, a single NASA launch of the space shuttle to the International Space Station (ISS) cost around $300 million and involved the work of more than ten thousand people. When Musk entered the space business, only the United States, China, Russia, India, and the European Union had the technical prowess and massive wealth needed for such projects.

Musk, with his nontraditional way of looking at things, believed he could devise cheaper, more efficient methods for building rockets and space capsules. After spending long hours on rocket research he discovered something: Rocket technology had not improved since the 1960s. This was due to the fact that the company that supplied rockets to NASA, called Orbital Sciences, was afraid to take risks. Rather than design a new style of rocket engine, which might not work at first, costing the company billions, it was cheaper to rely on old technology that had worked in the past. As Musk describes it:

Orbital Sciences has a contract to resupply the International Space Station, and their rocket honestly sounds like the punch line to a joke. It uses Russian rocket engines that were made in the '60s. I don't mean their design is from the '60s—I mean they start with engines that were *literally* made in the '60s and, like, packed away in Siberia [northern Russia] somewhere.[37]

New Look at an Old Idea

Musk was not afraid to take risks, and he saw a market for rockets updated for the twenty-first century. And while he was not a rocket

The International Space Station

The International Space Station (ISS) has been orbiting about 220 miles (354 km) above Earth since 1998. The first astronauts arrived in 2000, and the ISS has been inhabited ever since. Over time, new pieces of the ISS were ferried from Earth, and the entire space station was completed in 2011. Elon Musk's company SpaceX began servicing the ISS in 2012, transporting food, water, and experiments to its residents.

The ISS weighs around 1 million pounds (453,592 kg), is about the size of a five-bedroom house, and contains two bathrooms, a gym, and a large bay window. It houses six people at a time. The ISS has science labs from the United States, Russia, Japan, and European countries. The experiments and research conducted there will one day be used to plan crewed missions to the Moon, Mars, and possibly beyond.

The ISS is powered by two large banks of solar panels, called solar array wings, that collect energy from the Sun. Each wing uses nearly 33,000 solar cells and is 115 feet (35 meters) in length and 39 feet (12 meters) wide. The outer structure also contains robot arms that are used to build and repair the space station as well as move astronauts around in space as they perform maintenance and conduct experiments.

engineer, he had a unique background that helped him address the problems in front of him. As Musk explains:

> I grew up in sort of an engineering environment—my father is an electromechanical engineer. And so there were lots of engineery things around me. When I asked for an explanation, I got the true explanation of how things work. I also did things like make model rockets, and in South Africa there were no premade rockets: I had to go to the chemist and get the ingredients for rocket fuel, mix it, put it in a pipe.[38]

Musk delved into astronautical engineering and began the process of designing his first rocket. It would be named Falcon 1 after the *Millennium Falcon* spacecraft in one of Musk's favorite films, *Star Wars.*

"I grew up in sort of an engineering environment— my father is an electro- mechanical engineer. And so there were lots of engineery things around me."[38]

—Elon Musk.

Musk determined that rockets are made from basic materials like aluminum alloys, titanium, copper, and carbon fiber. He decided he could assemble these materials and build the Falcon 1 for around $7 million. The value of these materials on the open market was only about 2 percent of the price NASA paid for a typical rocket. By comparison, the materials in a car make up about 25 percent of the sale price. Musk would also save money by keeping his company small and efficient; NASA and Orbital Sciences had many layers of bureaucracy, which slowed projects while driving up costs.

Musk planned to save the most money by doing something no one had ever done before—using rockets more than one time. Traditionally, rockets are built in two or more stages. Each stage contains its own engine and fuel. After a rocket is launched, the first stage burns for about two minutes, separates, and plunges into the ocean. The second stage then fires, burns for several minutes, and pushes the rocket farther into space before running out of fuel and falling away. The complex, expensive engines are rarely recovered after their single use. As Musk views the process: "Throwing away multimillion-dollar rocket stages every flight makes no more sense than chucking away a 747 after every flight."[39] With this in mind, Musk planned to fish Falcon 1s out of the ocean after each launch. His long-range plans involved building a rocket that could land in a controlled manner, like an airplane or helicopter.

Just a Container for Fuel

Musk understood that a rocket on paper was far different from the real thing. Rockets fly at speeds of around 6,000 miles per hour (9,656 kph). The body of the craft, or airframe, must survive intense heat, cold, and pressure, forces in the atmosphere that can tear a rocket apart.

Rockets like the planned Falcon 1, with liquid-fuel engines, carry into space payloads such as communications satellites or spacecraft. To do so they need over 1 million pounds (453,592 kg) of rocket-grade kerosene and liquid oxygen fuel. When these two elements are combined and ignited, they create a high-pressure and high-velocity stream of hot gases that flow through a nozzle that accelerates them further. This creates enough thrust to push the 4.5-million-pound rocket (2 million kg) into space. However, in Musk's mind this complex machine was easy to understand: "If you think about it, a rocket is really just a container for the liquid oxygen and fuel—it's a combination propellant tank and primary airframe."[40]

As SpaceX engineers worked to design and build the first 70-foot-long Falcon 1 (21 m) from the ground up, the optimistic Musk lined up millions of dollars of launch contracts. And once again Musk managed to find an unmet need at an opportune time.

In 2004 NASA was launching the space shuttle three to four times a year to ferry astronauts and supplies to the International Space Station, which was still being assembled in outer space. NASA wanted to end its involvement with the ISS project. NASA picked SpaceX over its competitors to take over the space shuttle missions. But first Musk would have to prove to NASA that the Falcon 1 was safe and reliable; this proved to be more difficult than even Musk expected.

In 2004 NASA selected Musk's company SpaceX to take over deliveries between Earth and the International Space Station (pictured).

Relief Not Elation

In 2004 Musk signed a $15-million-dollar contract with the Department of Defense to use a Falcon 1 to deliver an experimental military satellite called TacSat-1 into orbit. The satellite was designed to provide ground imagery to military commanders waging war in Afghanistan, Iraq, and elsewhere. Due to technical problems the launch never took place, and the mission was canceled. In the years that followed, SpaceX attempted several other unsuccessful launches for the military.

After another failed mission in August 2008, Musk badly needed a win: Critics had already pronounced SpaceX dead. Musk got his victory on September 28 as the Falcon 1 rode a long column of burning fuel out of the atmosphere and into the history books; it was the first successful orbital launch of any privately funded and developed liquid-propelled rocket. After three major failures costing millions of dollars and threatening the existence of SpaceX, Musk told reporters: "That was freakin' awesome. It's great to have this giant monkey off my back. It's been six years of extremely intense effort and some pretty heart-wrenching episodes during prior launches. The emotion I feel is much more relief than elation. . . . It really gives a huge kick in the [groin] to the naysayers."[41]

Going Up in a Dragon

Even as Musk celebrated his victory, engineers at SpaceX were working intensely to build and develop the Falcon 9 launch vehicle. The second-generation Falcon was 173 feet (53 m) in length, nearly two-and-a-half times the size of the Falcon 1. It was also much more expensive, with an expected cost of around $55 million per launch. However, Musk did not have to finance this rocket himself. Development of the Falcon 9 was paid for by NASA's Commercial Orbital Transportation Services (COTS) program. This program was created in January 2006 with the goal of funding private companies to deliver crew and cargo to the International Space Station.

In 2006 COTS provided SpaceX with $278 million to fund three Falcon 9 demonstration flights. If these were successful, SpaceX would receive an additional $1.6 billion for twelve missions to the ISS. For these missions SpaceX would have to do more than build dependable rockets. The company would also have to provide a spacecraft, a vehicle designed to enter outer space, travel to the ISS, and return safely to Earth. So while one team of SpaceX engineers worked on the Falcon 9, another developed the spacecraft that Musk named Dragon.

"Throwing away multimillion-dollar rocket stages every flight makes no more sense than chucking away a 747 after every flight."[39]

—Elon Musk.

While Musk mocked the 1960s Russian rocket engines used by Orbital Sciences, he looked back to the sixties when designing Dragon. Unlike NASA's sleek Space Shuttle, which resembles a large passenger jet, the Dragon looks like the type of space capsule that carried American astronauts into orbit in the mid-1960s. Resembling a shuttlecock used in badminton, the Dragon was a blunt-nosed capsule around 12 feet (3.7 m) wide. Musk did not care what the Dragon looked like; he just wanted to make sure it had a window so astronauts, including himself, could see the stars when they flew in it. As he said, "I would like to go up in a Dragon at some point. A few years after its first flying. I think it would be great, huge amounts of fun. A very life-changing experience."[42]

SpaceX Makes a Difference

On Friday, June 4, 2010, Musk took one step toward his goal of going up in a Dragon. After hours of delay the first Falcon 9 flight streaked into the clear blue skies above Cape Canaveral in Florida. The rocket was carrying a mockup of the Dragon capsule, which was placed into orbit 155 miles (250 km) above Earth. Later in the day Musk told reporters that the Falcon 9 hit a "near bull's-eye, [which made Friday] one of the greatest days of my life. . . . It shows that even a sort of small new company like SpaceX can make a real difference."[43] There were a few glitches, however. Although SpaceX engineers planned to recover the first stage of the rocket they could not. The Falcon 9 broke up upon reentry into the atmosphere when its parachutes did not open properly.

Unlike the Falcon 1, with its three failures, the Falcon 9 flew almost flawlessly from the start. The second launch of the rocket on December 8, 2010, carried a Dragon spacecraft that orbited Earth two times and splashed down in the Pacific Ocean. Four months later NASA retired the Space Shuttle program.

On May 21, 2012, the Dragon was used for the first time to resupply the International Space Station. With this historic mission the Dragon became the first commercial spacecraft to visit the ISS. Another Dragon mission was carried out in September. On this mission the spacecraft transported elements needed for about 225 scientific experiments being conducted aboard the ISS. The Dragon also carried a 3D printer that was used to test whether astronauts could produce their own spare parts, tools, and even food.

"Close but No Cigar"

On September 29, 2013, SpaceX launched a new rocket Musk called Falcon 9 v1.1 (this replaced what was now called the Falcon 9 v1.0). The v1.1 was 224 feet (68.4 m) in length and 60 percent more powerful than the original Falcon 9. On its first mission the upgraded Falcon 9 carried CASSIOPE, a small communications and research satellite, into orbit for the Canadian Space Agency.

In the months that followed the launch, SpaceX experimented with methods for recovering and reusing the first stage of the Falcon 9. The experiments were called post-mission, controlled-descent tests. In theory, the Falcon 9's rocket engines could be fired at low power in what was called a reentry burn. This was meant to slow the stage as it fell back to Earth. As the rocket approached Earth's surface, landing legs would be deployed. The power of the rocket engines would then be slowly decreased in what was called a landing burn. This would steer the stage to the landing target and allow it to softly touch down.

When the first SpaceX launch of 2015 was announced, Musk planned to put the experiments with reentry burns and landing legs to use in what he hoped would be a noteworthy day for reusable rocket technology. In a risky effort, which Musk estimated had only a 50 percent chance of success, SpaceX would attempt to achieve a soft landing with the first stage. It would touch down on what Musk called an autonomous spaceport drone ship. This was a platform 300 feet long by 170 feet wide (91 m by 52 m) floating in the Atlantic Ocean. Musk describes the difficulties involved: "During previous attempts, we could only expect a landing accuracy of within 10 kilometers (6.2 miles). For this attempt, we're targeting a landing accuracy of within 10 meters (33 feet). [Doing this will be like] trying to balance a rubber broomstick on your hand in the middle of a wind storm."[44]

On January 10, 2015, the Falcon 9 delivered a Dragon spacecraft into orbit to resupply the ISS. When the first stage ran out of fuel, SpaceX engineers steered it toward the spaceport drone ship. However, the soft landing SpaceX hoped for was not to be. As Musk tweeted shortly after the mission: "Rocket made it to drone spaceport ship, but landed hard. Close, but no cigar this time. Bodes well for the future tho. Ship itself is fine. Some of the support equipment on the deck will need to be replaced."[45]

SpaceX released a dramatic video several days after the failed soft-landing attempt. The first stage of the rocket, as tall as a fourteen-story building, is seen hitting the drone ship at a forty-five-degree angle.

The Falcon 9 rocket is launched from Cape Canaveral in Florida in early 2015.

Engineers try to restore the fast-moving rocket's balance by firing its engines, which shoot columns of fire. This attempt fails to right the rocket. It skids across the deck of the ship and plunges into the sea. Large chunks of the rocket tumble chaotically across the deck in what Musk humorously called a "full RUD (rapid unscheduled disassembly) event."[46]

Despite the rocket's rapid disassembly, simply steering it onto the ship was a major accomplishment. And the crash was caused by a relatively minor problem; the hydraulic fluid that controlled the rocket's stabilizing fins ran out right before the landing. Musk announced he would try a second soft landing with 50 percent more hydraulic fluid to control the fins.

Making Life Multi-Planetary

Several months before the flaming Falcon crash landing, Musk told students at the Massachusetts Institute of Technology (MIT), "Reusability is the critical breakthrough needed in rocketry to take things to the next level."[47] To Musk, the next level involved getting contracts with the Department of Defense, which was scheduled to spend $70 billion on satellite launches before 2030. Musk planned to take the profits from these launches to fund missions to Mars. The goal was to eventually establish a populated colony on the red planet.

Musk was driven to undertake such a task because he believes what he calls the "light of consciousness"[48] is rare in the universe. He fears that climate change or nuclear war might someday make Earth uninhabitable. And Musk feels the effort to take humanity beyond Earth is as important as wiping out poverty or curing disease:

> I think there is a strong humanitarian argument for making life multi-planetary in order to safeguard the existence of humanity in the event that something catastrophic were to happen, in which case being poor or having a disease would be irrelevant, because humanity would be extinct. It would be like, "Good news, the problems of poverty and disease have been solved, but the bad news is there aren't any humans left."[49]

Organizing a crewed mission to Mars is no simple feat. At its closest orbit, Mars is 36 million miles (58 million km) from Earth. This is 150 times farther than the distance to the Moon. Depending on the speed of the launch and the alignment of Earth and Mars, the journey could take between 150 and 300 days in spacecraft traveling at approximately 12,400 miles per hour (19,955 kph). Any space vehicle making such a journey would have to carry people, food, water, oxygen, and shelter. Most important, the spacecraft would need to carry fuel that would make up about 80 percent of the vehicle's weight. A nuclear- or electric-powered space vehicle might solve the fuel problem, but no such entity currently exists.

A Million People on Mars

Musk is not bothered by seemingly insurmountable problems. He believes a colony on Mars will be functioning by 2040, and tens of thousands or even a million people will live there. Musk explained the logistics of such a mission:

> If you could take 100 people at a time, you would need 10,000 trips to get to a million people. But you would also need a lot of cargo to support those people. In fact, your cargo to person ratio is going to be quite high. It would probably be 10 cargo trips for every human trip, so more like 100,000 trips. And we're talking 100,000 trips of a giant spaceship.[50]

Life on Mars would be somber. The planet is often enveloped in massive dust storms, and Martian residents would be subjected to dangerous levels of cosmic radiation. Mars dwellers would most likely live in underground caves in very confined quarters; they would never feel the sun or wind on their skin. Earth would be visible only through a high-powered telescope. Despite the drawbacks Musk believes people will pay good money, up to a million dollars, for a one-way ticket to Mars. And he wants to be there with them. As Musk stated in 2013: "Space travel is the best thing we can do to extend the life of humanity. . . . I will go if I can be assured that SpaceX would go on without me. . . . I want to die on Mars, just not on impact."[51]

"I want to die on Mars, just not on impact."[51]

—Elon Musk.

Mind on Mars

An interplanetary mission to Mars would easily be the most expensive and challenging engineering project ever undertaken. But much closer

Obstacles to a Colony on Mars

Elon Musk breezily speaks of sending thousands of people to [...] few decades. However, many obstacles would need to be overcome to carry out such a grand mission. People would have to survive a 150- to 300-day spaceflight and land safely on Mars. They would need the means to survive in the harsh Martian landscape, which can boil the blood of an unprotected person in less than thirty seconds.

The main problem with a Mars colony involves soft-landing a rocket on the surface of the planet, where there is little atmosphere. On Earth the atmosphere provides friction, which slows a spacecraft during landing. On Mars the atmosphere is so thin it would not slow down a craft enough for a soft landing, even if the capsule had huge parachutes.

Surviving in a colony on Mars has its own seemingly insurmountable problems. The population would need a constant supply of water, food, oxygen, and even clean clothes from Earth; the International Space Station is supplied by three or four flights a year, and it is six times closer than Mars. If 100,000 people lived on Mars, as Musk proposed, supply ships would have to leave Earth every day, travel for nearly a year to Mars—and then make the journey home.

Solar radiation is also a great risk to astronauts. People living on Mars for a year or two would have an extra risk of cancer, which could shorten their lives by fifteen years. Traveling on the Martian surface in a vehicle or working in a greenhouse would further increase exposure to cosmic radiation. Scientists compare this risk of cancer to living on Earth immediately after a nuclear war.

to Earth, Musk moved to combine his love of space with the Internet. In January 2015 he opened an office in Seattle where around sixty engineers worked to develop what are called mini-satellites. These communications satellites, which could be built on an assembly line, would weigh less than 250 pounds (113 kg) and cost around $350,000 each. By omparison, current satellites weigh 25,000 to 40,000 pounds (11,340 to 18,143 kg), take years to manufacture, and cost tens of millions of dollars each. Up to seven hundred mini-satellites would be put into orbit together. They would be used to provide global, low-cost Internet access to people everywhere, including the poor living in remote locations.

Musk's mini-satellite project is expected to cost around $1 billion. As with his other ventures, experts expressed doubts about its probability and profitability. But Musk thinks big, and those who underestimate him have been proved wrong time and again.

Chapter 4

Tesla Motors

When Elon Musk was still a college student in the early 1990s he often worried about the environmental problems caused by automobiles. Then, as now, cars and trucks were the single largest source of air pollution in the United States and many other countries. Musk also worried that oil reserves would someday run dry, and there were no plans for replacing gasoline- and diesel-fueled engines. Musk believed electric cars were the first step toward moving society away from oil-based transportation. And he was so focused on the idea that the first question he asked on a first date was, "What do you think of electric cars?"[52]

More than a decade later, in 2002, Musk remained fascinated by electric cars even as he was founding his space transportation company SpaceX. While starting a rocket manufacturing company might be enough work for some, Musk decided to build electric cars. On July 2003, one year and one month after incorporating SpaceX, Musk launched Tesla Motors in Fremont, California, using $30 million of his own money. The company was named after the renowned Serbian electrical engineer Nikola Tesla, who is credited with inventing the alternating current (AC) electrical motor in the 1880s. According to Tesla Motors spokeswoman Rachel Konrad, "The Tesla Roadster uses an AC motor descended directly from Tesla's original 1882 design, which he said came to him in a vision."[53]

Although Musk is also considered a visionary by some, few analysts believed he would find success in the car industry. Starting an automobile company is a high-risk proposition; there has not been a successful startup car company in the United States since Walter P. Chrysler began producing the eponymous Chrysler automobiles in 1924. After World War II the auto startup Kaiser Motors made cars for eight years

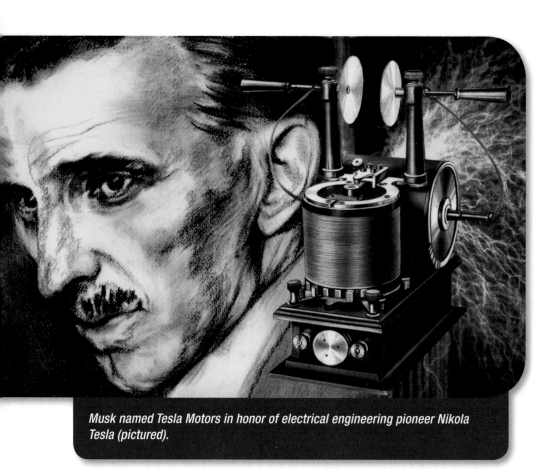

Musk named Tesla Motors in honor of electrical engineering pioneer Nikola Tesla (pictured).

before declaring bankruptcy in 1955. In 1975 the auto company Delorean produced only nine thousand of its futuristic sports cars before running out of money. By the time Musk founded Tesla, the auto industry was dominated by Ford, General Motors (GM), Chrysler, and major German, Japanese, and Korean companies. However, Musk believed he could compete with the auto giants by producing highway-capable, all-electric vehicles powered by rechargeable batteries.

The EV1

Electric cars are not a new concept. In 1900 nearly 40 percent of all cars in the United States were battery powered. However, a 1901 Texas oil boom made gasoline so cheap and plentiful that within a few years gas-burning internal combustion vehicles dominated the marketplace.

Electric cars made a minor comeback between 1996 and 1999 when GM produced a battery-powered car called the EV1. About two thousand EV1s were leased to select customers at a cost of $250 to $500 a month. However, the cars were very expensive to produce; the entire EV1 program cost GM about $1 billion.

GM stopped producing EV1s in 1999, and when the leases expired in 2003 the company recalled all the electric cars. They were taken to a junkyard in Arizona and crushed into scrap metal while fans of the EV1 lit candles in protest outside the gates. When asked about the EV1 in 2014, Musk stated that the car was part of his inspiration for building electric automobiles. And he said that GM should never have scrapped its electric car program. According to Musk: "They should have gone to EV2 and EV3 . . . making it better. The EV1 was not a great car. It had a lot of issues. But it was good enough to encourage people to take extraordinary steps to try to keep it and to hold candle-lit vigils when it was crushed. They don't do that for other GM products."[54]

Musk saw several problems with the EV1. Most obvious was its clunky design; with its bulbous front end and rounded contours, the car looked like something that might have rolled off the GM assembly line in the 1980s. The second problem was more critical. During its first few years of production the EV1 was powered by lead-acid batteries. These are the same type of batteries used to start the engines of gasoline-fueled cars. The lead-acid batteries in the early EV1s took eight hours to recharge and had a range of only 60 to 100 miles (97 to 161 km). Few Americans were willing to lease an expensive car that could travel only a short distance between long charges.

The Roadster Is Born

Musk had a better idea for an electric car that would grab the public's attention, and in March 2004 the Tesla Roadster was born. This was no bulky GM coupe built with old technology. The Roadster was a flashy two-seat electric sports car. The body panels were constructed from a carbon fiber material, an expensive, extremely strong, lightweight material used on high-end luxury cars and jet airliners.

The first Tesla Roadster was shown to the public in July 2006 at an invitation-only unveiling in Santa Monica, California. In the months that followed, the Roadster made the rounds of various auto shows across the country.

The Roadster's design was loosely based on the Lotus Elise, an exotic British sports car. It was the first car ever powered by lithium-ion (Li-ion) batteries such as those used in cell phones and laptop computers. The batteries could be fully recharged in around four hours, and they provided the Roadster with a record-setting travel range of 244 miles (393 km).

The first highway-ready Roadster to roll off production lines was delivered to Musk in February 2008. Five hundred more Roadsters were produced that year and sold at a cost of $100,000. Tesla Roadsters were purchased by a who's who of celebrities including actors George Clooney, Matt Damon, and Leonardo DiCaprio; rock stars Michael "Flea" Balzary and Anthony Kiedis of the Red Hot Chili Peppers; and Google founders Sergey Brin and Larry Page.

Roadster buyers were attracted to the car's environmental credentials as well as its silent motor, which takes the car from 0 to 60 mph (96 kph) in 3.9 seconds. This rapid acceleration made the Roadster as fast, if not faster, than Porsches, Ferraris, and other ultra-high-end sports cars. As Musk told reporters in June 2008: "I think anyone who likes fast cars will love the Tesla. And it has fantastic handling by the way. I mean this car will crush a Porsche on the track, just crush it. . . . And then oh, by the way, it happens to be electric and it's twice the efficiency of a Prius [Toyota's gas-electric hybrid].[55]

> "I think anyone who likes fast cars will love the Tesla. . . . I mean this car will crush a Porsche on the track, just crush it."[55]
>
> —Elon Musk.

According to Tesla figures, the Roadster produced half the carbon dioxide (CO_2) of a Prius. And although the car was fully electric, its energy consumption was the equivalent of 120 miles per gallon (2 L per 100 km). A Prius was rated at about 50 miles per gallon (4.7 L per 80 km). In 2008 it cost about four dollars to fully charge the Roadster at a time when gas was selling for four dollars a gallon in California.

In 2009 the Tesla Roadster set the world distance record for an electric car, traveling 311 miles (510 km) on a single charge. By 2012 Tesla had sold about twenty-five hundred Roadsters in thirty-one countries.

The Model S

Musk's plans went beyond producing an expensive, exclusive electric car. He wanted to use the profits from the Roadster to build a more affordable car. As he blogged before the Roadster's release: "I can say that the second model will be a sporty four door family car at roughly half the [price] of the Tesla Roadster, and the third model will be even more affordable."[56] However, things did not quite work out as planned for the second model. When the all-aluminum four-door Tesla Model S went on sale in June 2012, the base price was $70,000. And the price of

A worker assembles a Tesla Model S. The car went on sale in June 2012.

the Model S could exceed $95,000 if purchased with the longest-range batteries.

Whatever its cost, the beautifully styled Model S was unique in many ways. The Model S was bigger and heavier than the Roadster, it seated four, and was just as fast. The base Model S promised a range of 208 miles (335 km), while the top-of-the-line model could go 265 miles (426 km) on a single charge.

Style and performance aside, the Model S was like no other car. The rear hatchback cargo compartment could be fitted with two rear-facing child seats. Anyone lifting the front hood would find a large, deep cargo compartment where a motor and transmission would be located in other cars. Compact electric motors were placed at both the front and rear axles, and a slab of Li-ion batteries was placed under the entire interior floor space.

The recessed outer door handles of the Model S were made to slide out as a driver approached with a key fob. Inside, every task from adjusting the climate control to popping open the trunk was handled by a flat-panel touchscreen display in the center of the dash. Such simple, elegant features thrilled auto reviewers. The respected *Consumer Reports* magazine gave the Model S high marks for safety and reliability.

In 2014 Tesla introduced an upgraded Model S, called a P85D. And the car was even faster, reaching 60 mph (96 kph) from a standing stop in only 3.2 seconds. Musk called the P85D, "The World's Fastest Accelerating Four-door Production Car," but achieving that title was not easy: "We already had enough fish to fry just making a car that worked. But it was always something we expected to do. We wanted to position it as the fastest in order to change the public mindset. It had to be something dramatic. And getting those few extra 10ths of a second was hard."[57]

SolarCity

Despite the engineering triumph of the P85D, not everyone loved the Model S. Environmentalists noted that with a cost of nearly $100,000 the Tesla was too expensive to provide a practical solution to climate change. In addition, electricity is produced by coal in many states, particularly in the East and South. If a Tesla battery is recharged from a coal-fired power plant it produces as much CO_2 per mile as a $30,000 gas-powered Honda Accord.

Musk was aware of this problem and addressed it with a high-profile solution. In 2012 he founded the solar energy company SolarCity, based in San Mateo, California. Musk's cousins, Peter Rive and Lyndon Rive, ran the company. The main objective of SolarCity was to build what Musk called Superchargers. These solar-powered fast-charging stations for electric vehicles were installed along major highways throughout North America. A thirty-minute charge at a Supercharger extends the range of a Tesla Model S an additional 170 miles (373 km).

In 2015 there were 119 Supercharger solar stations in the United States and a dozen in western Canada. In addition, 83 Superchargers were built in Europe and 20 in Asia. Tesla owners could use them for free.

Making Supercharging Easy

Elon Musk made sure his charging stations were time-efficient as well as easy to use. If drivers do not have time to wait thirty or forty minutes for a charge, they can opt to have their depleted battery pack swapped with a freshly charged one. The operation takes less than ninety seconds and costs about sixty dollars. Owners can pick up their original battery pack, freshly charged, on the return trip.

In February 2014 Tesla Motors set out to show how easy Supercharging can be. A team of fifteen drivers, a pair of Tesla Model S cars, and a gas-powered support car completed a cross-country trip from Los Angeles to New York City, detouring north through Minnesota and South Dakota where temperatures were -4°F (-20°C). The team, using nothing but Supercharger power, made the 3,464-mile nonstop journey (5,575 km) in seventy-six hours. The only glitch—the gas-powered car broke down. A month after the Tesla team made the journey, Musk and his family took a similar trip for a cross-country vacation.

Most Superchargers were located near restaurants and shopping centers. Musk promised that within a few years there would be double the number of Superchargers along well-traveled highways in North America and elsewhere.

Calming Range Anxiety

The Superchargers were meant to address what is called "range anxiety." This is the fear that an electric car will run out of power before it reaches its destination. According to a December 2013 survey by the Union of Concerned Scientists, half of all drivers polled said they would not buy or lease an electric car because of range anxiety.

In March 2014 Musk set out on a high-profile journey to put an end to range anxiety. He took a cross-country trip in a Tesla with his five children. Musk was also accompanied by second wife, actress Talulah Riley. The couple married in 2008 after Musk divorced his first wife, Justine. Talulah called the journey "The Great American (Electric) Road-trip."[58]

Musk's 3,200-mile journey (5,150 km) from Los Angeles to New York City took six days. Unlike most families on a cross-country trip, the Musks were accompanied by five security guards and, in case of breakdowns, a large Chevy Suburban SUV. During the trip, a total of nine hours was spent at twenty different Supercharging stations. A driver in a gas-powered Toyota Camry making the same trip would need to stop to fill the tank less than half that number of times. However, as Musk tweeted, he stopped only to charge the Tesla while the family was engaged in other activities: "At 1.5 hrs/day, we will only ever need to charge when stopping anyway to eat or sightsee, never just for charging itself."[59]

The Gigafactory

By the time Musk had traveled across the United States, total sales of the Model S were nearing the fifty thousand mark. And Musk remained highly optimistic about the Tesla's prospects. He promised to sell five hundred thousand of the Model S by 2020 and several million by 2025. Musk also vowed to begin production of a more affordable car in 2015, a $35,000

Elon Musk announces plans to build a facility known as a "Gigafactory," where batteries to power Tesla automobiles will be produced.

electric sedan called the Model 3 (or Model III). However, production was delayed numerous times, and the launch date was pushed back to 2017.

Part of the challenge in producing a low-cost electric car concerns the high cost of purchasing Li-ion batteries from other producers. To deal with this problem Musk decided to open his third major production facility.

In September 2014 he broke ground on a $5 billion Li-ion battery factory outside Reno, Nevada.

Musk labeled the battery production facility a Gigafactory and revealed plans to power the building with renewable solar, wind, and geothermal energy. By producing its own batteries, Tesla would be able to lower the price of its cars. As Musk stated, without the Gigafactory, "we cannot produce a mass-market [electric] car."[60] When completed in 2017 the Gigafactory will be the biggest battery factory in the world, with the capacity to produce enough batteries to supply half a million vehicles.

In addition to building high-tech car batteries, the Gigafactory is scheduled to produce a new line of efficient, low-cost SolarCity home solar panels. Musk is a longtime proponent of solar energy and believes the power source could provide for all of the nation's electrical needs. As Musk told a group of engineers in Norway in 2014: "You could power the entire United States with about 150 to 200 square kilometers [58 to 77 sq. mi.] of solar panels, the entire United States. Take a corner of Utah [and install solar panels]. . . . There's not much going on there, I've been there."[61]

A Crazy Chemical Experiment

If Musk succeeds with his plans his customers will have no use for fossil fuels or traditional energy companies. They will be able to charge their Teslas with Superchargers on the highway and SolarCity rooftop solar panels at home.

While Musk's version of the future would undoubtedly add to his wealth, his main motivation was to slow climate change. As Musk explained in 2013, he thought it was insane to base the world's economy on fossil fuels (hydrocarbons), which are warming the planet:

> I think currently that what we're doing right now, which is mining and burning trillions of tons of hydrocarbons that used to be buried very deep underground, and now we're sticking them in the atmosphere and running this crazy chemical experiment on the atmosphere. And then we've got the oil and gas companies that have ungodly amounts of money. You can't expect them to

roll over and die. . . . [But] what's the percentage chance that this could be catastrophic for some meaningful percentage of earth's population? Is it greater than 1%? Is it even 1%? If it is even 1%, why are we running this experiment? . . . It's the world's dumbest experiment.[62]

Freeing Up Technology

Musk further demonstrated his commitment to slowing climate change in June 2014 when he offered to give away Tesla's patented technology to other auto makers for free. This was seen as a controversial move; a patent is a set of exclusive rights granted to an inventor for what is called intellectual property. When Musk designed the first Teslas he secured patents on the car's unique propulsion systems to prevent large auto makers such as Toyota and BMW from using his trade secrets in their own electric cars.

> "[We're] burning trillions of tons of hydrocarbons that used to be buried very deep underground, and now we're sticking them in the atmosphere and running this crazy chemical experiment on the atmosphere."[62]
>
> —Elon Musk.

Musk soon realized auto industry giants were not that interested in the Tesla. Disappointed by what he called their "small to non-existent" investments in electric cars, Musk released his patent rights to stimulate development of a larger electric vehicle industry. As Musk writes in his blog: "If we clear a path to the creation of electric vehicles, but then lay intellectual property landmines behind us to inhibit others, we are acting in a manner contrary to that goal. Tesla will not initiate patent lawsuits against anyone who, in good faith, wants to use our technology."[63]

Musk had even greater plans for "green" transportation. In January 2015 he announced plans to build a 5-mile test track (8 km) in Texas for what he calls the Hyperloop. This revolutionary high-speed, mass-transport system would whisk travelers in a sealed tube between Los Angeles and San Francisco at the speed of 760 mph (1,220 kph). And the solar-powered Hyperloop between Los Angeles and San Francisco would be the first link in a national transportation system that could someday connect all major American cities.

The Hyperloop Alpha

In 2013 Elon Musk uploaded to Tesla and SpaceX websites the extensively detailed fifty-eight-page Hyperloop Alpha plan. The plan contained graphics, charts, and scientific design information for building a Hyperloop, a $6 billion mass-transit system between Los Angeles and San Francisco. The Hyperloop would consist of pods, each carrying twenty-eight passengers, zipping through a long, sealed tube constructed on pylons situated along Interstate 5. The pods would ride on a cushion of air at speeds of 760 mph (1,220 kph), making the 380-mile journey (611 km) in less than thirty minutes. As Musk described the Hyperloop:

> How would you like something that can never crash, is immune to weather, it goes 3 or 4 times faster than the bullet train. It goes an average speed of twice what an aircraft would do. You would go from downtown LA to downtown San Francisco in under 30 minutes. . . . I think we could actually make it self-powering if you put solar panels on it, you generate more power than you would consume in the system. There's a way to store the power so it would run 24/7 without using batteries. Yes, this is possible, absolutely.

Quoted in Jay Yarow, "How Elon Musk Could Change the World with a High-Speed Transportation System Called the Hyperloop," *Business Insider*, July 15, 2013. www.businessinsider.com.

Humanity's Future

While Musk made futuristic plans, he was not always optimistic about what the future might hold. He often voiced warnings about robots equipped with artificial intelligence, or AI. In a scenario straight out of a science fiction novel, Musk expressed fears that robots designed to think and reason like people might someday enslave humanity. As he told students in a 2014 speech at the Massachusetts Institute of Technology (MIT):

I think we should be very careful about artificial intelligence. If I had to guess at what [the biggest threat to our existence] is, it's probably that. So we need to be very careful. I'm increasingly inclined to think that there should be some regulatory oversight, maybe at the national and international level, just to make sure that we don't do something very foolish.[64]

Musk's comments generated criticism among AI proponents who mocked him for what they called his fear of killer robots. Musk was also accused of hypocrisy; he was one of the original investors in an AI firm called Vicarious, a company working to build a computer that could think like a person. The machine would have software that mimicked the part of the brain that controls vision, body movement, and language. Musk answered his critics by stating that he invested in the company to keep an eye on what was going on and to stop any potentially dangerous outcomes.

Foundations and Awards

Whatever Musk's vision of the future, he understands that a new generation of scientists and engineers will be leading the way. In order to assist this new crop of designers, builders, and scientists, he started the Musk Foundation with his brother, Kimbal. The organization provides around half a million dollars in grants annually in support of science and engineering education, renewable energy research, space exploration, and pediatric research. In addition, the Musk Foundation donates solar power systems to areas hit by disaster. After a massive tidal wave wiped out Soma City in Fukushima, Japan, SolarCity provided the city with a $250,000 renewable energy facility.

Musk's charity and innovative companies have earned him numerous awards and recognition over the years. In 2013 he received the *Fortune* Businessperson of the Year Award for SpaceX, SolarCity, and Tesla Motors. The following year Musk earned the prestigious 2014 Edison Achievement Award for his lasting contributions to the world of innovation.

The Rock Star Entrepreneur

There is little doubt that Elon Musk wants to create a brighter future for humanity while simultaneously slowing climate change. But in a January 2014 interview, Musk also revealed that he is driven by his own need to be happy: "[I'm] inclined to say, 'How can we make things better?' And a lot of my motivation comes from me personally looking at things that don't work well and feeling a bit sad about how it would manifest in the future. And if that would result in an unhappy future, then it makes me unhappy. And so I want to fix it. That really is the motivation for me."[65]

> "A lot of my motivation comes from me personally looking at things that don't work well and feeling a bit sad about how it would manifest in the future."[65]
>
> —Elon Musk.

Due to his motivation and foresight Musk has been called a rock star entrepreneur. And it is said he provided inspiration for the character Tony Stark, the genius engineer in the blockbuster *Iron Man* movies. But Musk has not wavered in his vision despite the acquired trappings of fame and fortune. According to all accounts, Musk is a down-to-earth CEO who works as hard as his employees.

Musk's seemingly boundless genius and natural business sense created a successful electric car company and a network of highway Superchargers. All the while he oversaw the design, construction, and multiple launches of a new generation of rockets and spacecraft. Whether he did it for money or his own happiness is beside the point. Within a period of twenty years Musk's vision and energy helped transform the Internet, space travel, and even the way people can drive down the highway.

Source Notes

Introduction: Solving Problems for Humanity

1. Quoted in Alex Davies, "How Elon Musk Is Revolutionizing Two Major Industries at the Same Time," *Business Insider*, March 13, 2013. www.businessinsider.com.

2. Quoted in Ross Andersen, "Exodus," *Aeon*, September 30, 2014. http://aeon.co.

3. Quoted in Tom Junod, "Triumph of His Will," *Esquire*, November 15, 2012. www.esquire.com.

Chapter One: The Wonder Years

4. Quoted in Junod, "Triumph of His Will."

5. Quoted in Andrew Corsello, "The Believer," *GQ*, February 2009. www.gq.com.

6. Quoted in Junod, "Triumph of His Will."

7. Quoted in Junod, "Triumph of His Will."

8. Quoted in Ashlee Vance, "Elon Musk, the 21st Century Industrialist," *Bloomberg Business Weekly*, September 13, 2012. www.businessweek.com.

9. Quoted in David R. Baker, "Elon Musk, Future-of-Travel's New Disrupter-in-Chief," Skift, May 11, 2014. http://skift.com.

10. Quoted in BBC, "The Hitchhiker's Guide to the Galaxy: the Guide," June 18, 2014. www.bbc.co.uk.

11. Quoted in Vance, "Elon Musk, the 21st Century Industrialist."

12. Quoted in Ben Wattenberg, "Think Tank," PBS, 2014. www.pbs.org.

13. Quoted in Evan Carmichael, "The Wired Entrepreneur: The Early Years of Elon Musk," May 2014. www.evancarmichael.com.

14. Quoted in Junod, "Triumph of His Will."

15. Quoted in Vance, "Elon Musk, the 21st Century Industrialist."

16. Quoted in Evan Carmichael, "EBAY," May 2014. www.evancarmichael.com.

17. Elon Musk, "On Entrepreneurship," *Hacker Magazine*, July 2012. https://archive.org.

18. Quoted in Knowledge@Wharton, "Entrepreneur Elon Musk: Why It's Important to Pinch Pennies on the Road to Riches," May 27, 2009. http://knowledge.wharton.upenn.edu.

19. Quoted in Knowledge@Wharton, "Entrepreneur Elon Musk."

20. Quoted in Carmichael, "The Wired Entrepreneur."

21. Quoted in Carmichael, "The Wired Entrepreneur."

22. Justine Musk, "I Was a Starter Wife: Inside America's Messiest Divorce," *Marie Claire*, September 10, 2010. www.marieclaire.com.

Chapter Two: PayPal Payoff

23. Quoted in Karlin Lillington, "PayPal Puts Dough in Your Palm," *Wired*, July 27, 1999. http://archive.wired.com.

24. Lillington, "PayPal Puts Dough in Your Palm."

25. Musk, "On Entrepreneurship."

26. Musk, "On Entrepreneurship."

27. Quoted in Lisa Branstein, "Former Intuit CEO Harris Joins X.com," sec. B12, *Wall Street Journal*, December 7, 1999.

28. Eric M. Jackson, *The PayPal Wars*. Los Angeles: World Ahead, 2004, pp. 112–13.

29. Musk, "On Entrepreneurship."

30. Jackson, *The PayPal Wars*, pp. 169–70.

31. Jackson, *The PayPal Wars*, p. 182.

32. Jackson, *The PayPal Wars*, pp. 213–14.

33. Jackson, *The PayPal Wars*, pp. 218–19.

34. Quoted in Chris Anderson, "Elon Musk's Mission to Mars," *Wired*, October 10, 2012. www.wired.com.

35. Quoted in Chris Anderson, "Elon Musk's Mission to Mars."

36. Quoted in Josh Friedman, "Entrepreneur Tries His Midas Touch in Space," *Los Angeles Times*, April 22, 2003. http://articles.latimes.com.

37. Quoted in Chris Anderson, "Elon Musk's Mission to Mars."

38. Quoted in Chris Anderson, "Elon Musk's Mission to Mars."

39. Quoted in Leslie Wayne, "A Bold Plan to Go Where Men Have Gone Before," *New York Times*, February 5, 2006. www.nytimes.com.

40. Quoted in Chris Anderson, "Elon Musk's Mission to Mars."

41. Quoted in Stephen Clark, "Sweet Success at Last for Falcon 1 Rocket," Spaceflight Now, September 28, 2008. http://spaceflightnow.com.

42. Quoted in Paul Harris, "Elon Musk: 'I'm Planning to Retire to Mars,'" *Observer*, July 31, 2010. www.theguardian.com.

43. Quoted in Alan Boyle, "Shuttle Successor Succeeds in First Test Flight," NBC News, June 4, 2010. www.nbcnews.com.

44. Quoted in Jessica Orwig, "Saturday's SpaceX Launch Could Forever Change Spaceflight," *Business Insider*, January 5, 2015. www.businessinsider.com.

45. Quoted in Mike Wall, "Daring SpaceX Rocket Landing Test Crashes After Successful Cargo Launch for NASA," Space.com, January 10, 2015. www.space.com.

46. Quoted in Orwig, "Saturday's SpaceX Launch Could Forever Change Spaceflight."

47. Quoted in Orwig, "Saturday's SpaceX Launch Could Forever Change Spaceflight."

48. Quoted in Ross Andersen, "Exodus."

49. Quoted in Ross Andersen, "Exodus."

50. Quoted in Ross Andersen, "Exodus."

51. Quoted in Elien Blue Becque, "Elon Musk Wants to Die on Mars," *Vanity Fair*, March 10, 2013. www.vanityfair.com.

Chapter Four: Tesla Motors

52. Quoted in Daniel Alef, *Elon Musk: The X-Factor, Tesla and the Holy Grail*. Jersey City, NJ: Titans of Fortune, 2014, p. 392.

53. Quoted in Daniel Michaels, "Long-Dead Inventor Nikola Tesla Is Electrifying Hip Techies," *Wall Street Journal*, January 14, 2010. www.wsj.com.

54. Quoted in Jonathan Demacedo, "Tesla CEO Elon Musk Talks General Motors' Ill-Fated EV1," GM Authority, March 31, 2014. http://gmauthority.com.

55. Quoted in Spencer Michels, "Extended Interview: Tesla Motors Chairman Elon Musk," *Newshour*, PBS, June 25, 2008. www.pbs.org.

56. Quoted in Jerry Hirsch and Charles Fleming, "Ramping Up Production of Affordable Tesla May Take Years, Elon Musk Says," *Los Angeles Times*, January 13, 2015. www.latimes.com.

57. Quoted in Anthony Ffrench-Constant, "Elon Musk Talks Tesla," *GQ*, November 25, 2014. www.gq-magazine.co.uk.

58. Quoted in Seth Weintraub, "Elon Musk/Family Begins Cross Country Electric Road Trip," Electrek, March 31, 2014. http://electrek.co.

59. Quoted in Weintraub, "Elon Musk/Family Begins Cross Country Electric Road Trip."

60. Quoted in Julia Pyper, "Elon Musk's Tesla Picks Nevada to Host Battery Gigafactory," *Scientific American*, September 14, 2014. www.scientificamerican.com.

61. Quoted in Zachary Shahan, "5 Elon Musk Interviews, Tons of Awesome Quotes," Clean Technica, December 21, 2014, http://cleantechnica.com.

62. Quoted in Alison van Diggelen, "Elon Musk: On Obama, Climate Change & Government Regulation," Fresh Dialogues, February 11, 2013. www.freshdialogues.com.

63. Quoted in Alexander C. Kaufman, "Tesla Is Giving Away All of Its Ideas for Free," *Huffington Post*, June 13, 2014. www.huffingtonpost.com.

64. Quoted in Samuel Gibbs, "Elon Musk: Artificial Intelligence Is Our Biggest Existential Threat," *Guardian*, October 27, 2014. www.theguardian.com.

65. Quoted in Andrew Smith, "Meet Tech Billionaire and Real Life Iron Man Elon Musk," *Telegraph*, January 4, 2014. www.telegraph.co.uk.

Important Events in the Life of Elon Musk

June 28, 1971

Elon Reeve Musk is born in Pretoria, South Africa.

1981

Musk buys his first computer and learns to write code for programs and games.

1983

Musk designs a video game called "Blastar" and sells it for $500.

1988

Musk moves to Canada, his mother's native country.

1989

Musk attends Queen's University in Kingston, Ontario.

1992

Musk moves to the United States and attends the Wharton School of the University of Pennsylvania.

1994

Musk receives a bachelor's degree (BA) in economics from Wharton.

1995

Musk uses $4,000 to create Zip2, a company that converts printed media material into digital content.

1999

Zip2 is purchased by Compaq Computers for $300 million; Musk uses his $22 million share of the profits to start the online bank X.com.

2000

X.com buys Confinity, the company that becomes PayPal in 2001.

2002

eBay purchases PayPal for $1.5 billion with an estimated $180 million paid to Musk. He uses the money to found the space transportation company SpaceX.

2003

Musk launches Tesla Motors with $30 million of his own money.

2006

Musk unveils the first Tesla Roadster at a press conference in Santa Monica.

2008

On September 28 SpaceX successfully launches a Falcon 1 rocket into orbit, making it the first private company to achieve such a feat.

2009

The Tesla Roadster sets the world distance record for an electric car, traveling 311 miles (510 km) on a single charge.

2010

The first successful launch of a SpaceX Falcon 9 rocket takes place on June 4.

2012

On May 21, the SpaceX Dragon becomes the first commercial spacecraft to resupply the International Space Station.

2013

Musk makes public plans for the Hyperloop, a futuristic mass-transportation system that could whisk passengers in pods through a sealed tube at speeds of 760 mph (1,220 kph).

2014

Tesla introduces the P85D, "The World's Fastest Accelerating Four-Door Production Car."

For Further Research

Books

L.E. Carmichael, *Hybrid and Electric Vehicles*. Edina, MN: Abdo, 2013.

Caitlin Denham and Carla Mooney, *ROCKETRY: Investigate the Science and Technology of Rockets and Ballistics*. White River Junction, VT: Nomad, 2014.

Louise Gerdes, *Hybrid and Electric Cars*. Farmington Hills, MI: Greenhaven, 2014.

Shelley Tanaka, *Climate Change*. Revised Edition. Sydney, AU: Groundwood, 2013.

Websites

Green Car Reports (www.greencarreports.com). This website focuses on environmentally friendly cars and features videos, news, and blogs about e-car batteries, charging stations, and Elon Musk's latest vehicular ventures.

International Space Station (www.nasa.gov/mission_pages/station/main /index.htm). NASA's official website for the International Space Station, featuring photos, videos, and the latest news on landings, launches, and missions.

NASA Mars (http://mars.nasa.gov). NASA has been exploring Mars since the first spacecraft voyages took pictures of the red planet in 1965. This site covers NASA's Mars missions, technology, rovers, and the scientists behind the scenes.

60 Minutes (www.cbsnews.com/news/tesla-and-spacex-elon-musks -industrial-empire). The *60 Minutes* piece on Elon Musk, broadcast in March 2014, contains a complete transcript of the show plus extra video segments on Musk's family history and his endeavors with SpaceX and Tesla.

SpaceX (www.spacex.com). The official site of Elon Musk's space transportation company features the latest news, photos, and videos of SpaceX rocket and spacecraft designs, launches, and landings.

Tesla Motors (www.teslamotors.com). The website for Tesla electric automobiles presents facts, figures, diagrams, and videos of various models along with information about Supercharger charging stations.

Internet Sources

Stephen Clark, "SpaceX Shares Dramatic Video of Falcon 9's Crash Landing," Spaceflight Now, January 16, 2015. http://spaceflightnow.com /2015/01/16/elon-musk-shares-images-of-falcon-9s-crash-landing.

Adam Mann, "Why We Can't Send Humans to Mars Yet, and How We'll Fix That," *Wired*, May 31, 2013. www.wired.co.uk/news/archive/2013-05/31 /getting-to-mars.

Elon Musk, "Hyperloop Alpha," Tesla Motors, March 2013. www.tesla motors.com/sites/default/files/blog_images/hyperloop-alpha.pdf.

Films

Who Killed the Electric Car? Directed by Chris Paine. Hollywood, CA: Sony Pictures Classics, 2006, DVD.

Index

Note: Boldface page numbers indicate illustrations.

Adams, Douglas, 12
apartheid, 13–14
Arthur Dent (fictional character), 12
artificial intelligence (AI), 62–63
astronautical engineering, 38
automobile industry, overview of, 51–52
awards, 63

Bank One, 28
batteries
  in early cars, 53
  factory to produce, 59–60
  in first Roadster, 54
  in GM EV1, 53
  in Model S, 56–57
  supercapacitors and, 15
Bezos, Jeff, 6
Billpoint, 28, 35
Blastar (video game), 12
Brin, Sergey, 6
burn-rate, monetary 17, 30
businesses/enterprises
  Blastar, 12
  Gigafactory, 59–60
  party house at Wharton, 14–15
  SolarCity, 57–58, 60, 63
  Zip2, 8, 17–19
  See also PayPal; Space Exploration Technologies (SpaceX); Tesla Motors; X.com
Businessperson of the Year Award *(Fortune),* 63

Canada, 14
Canadian Space Agency, 45
cancer risks, 49
carbon dioxide, 7, 54
cars
  early battery-powered, 52–53
  and overview of industry, 51–52
  as polluters, 51
  See also Tesla Motors

CASSIOPE (satellite), 45
charity, 63
chess, 25
Chrysler, Walter P., 51
clean energy
  and gasoline and diesel vehicles as major polluters, 51
  as problem important to humanity, 15, 36, 56–58, 60
  production of electricity to charge batteries and, 56–57
  solar, 57–58, 60
  See also Tesla Motors
climate change and use of fossil fuels, 60–61
Commercial Orbital Transportation Services (COTS), 43
Commodore Vic20 (computer), 12
communications industry, 6, 8
computers
  Compaq, 18, 21
  early, 11–12
Confinity, 24, 27, 28
Consumer Reports (magazine), 56
consumer-to-consumer websites (C2C), 22–23

dot-com bubble, 20–21, 30
Dragon (spacecraft), 43–44

eBay
  creation and operation of, 22
  PayPal and, 26, 28, 30, 31, 33, 35
  PDAs for payment, 24
  popularity of, 23
  X.com and, 26
Edison Achievement Award, 63
electric cars
  as answer to gasoline and diesel vehicles, 51
  early, 52–53
  patents, 61
  pollution from charging, 56–57
  range anxiety and, 58
  solar-powered charging stations for, 57–58
  See also Tesla Motors

eMoneyMail, 28
EV1 (car), 53

Falcon 1 (rocket), 40, 41, 42–43
Falcon 9 (rocket), 43, 44–47, **46**

General Motors, 53
Gigafactory, 59–60
gMoney, 29

Haldeman, John Elon (great-grandfather), 9
Haldeman, Joshua (grandfather), 9
Harris, Bill, 26
Hitchhiker's Guide to the Galaxy, The (Adams),
   12
human longevity, 25
Hyperloop, 61–62

initial public offerings (IPOs), 33–35
intellectual property, 61
International Space Station (ISS), **42**
   flights to, annually, 49
   Orbital Sciences and, 38–39
   SpaceX and, 7, 39, 41, 44, 45
Internet
   as problem important to humanity, 15, 16,
      21, 36
   See also specific websites
Iron Man (films), 64

Jackson, Eric M.
   on customer service, 31–32
   on dot-com bubble burst, 30
   on Musk as hard worker, 32
   on PayPal working environment, 29
   on X.com competition with PayPal, 26–27
Jobs, Steve, 6

Kaiser Motors, 51–52
Konrad, Rachel, 51

lead-acid batteries, 53
Levchin, Max, 24, 29, 32–33
light of consciousness, 47
lithium-ion (Li-ion) batteries, 54, 56, 59–60
Lord of the Rings (Tolkien), 25

Mars, 47–50
Mars Oasis, 36–37, **37**
mini-satellites, 49–50

Musk, Elon Reeve, **7, 27, 59**
   on apartheid, 14
   on being US citizen, 13
   birth of, 9
   characteristics of, 11, 32, 64
   childhood of, 9–10
      on experiments during, 11, 40
      use of computers during, 12
   children of, 19–20
   education of, 10, 14–16, **16**
   on electric cars
      and affordability, 55
      and cross-country trip driving Model S,
         58
      and GM program, 53
      and need for Gigafactory, 60
      patents, 61
      and P85D, 56
      and Roadster as sports car, 54
   on fossil fuels, 60–61
   on future of humanity, 6, 7–8, 15, 36
   on goal of X.com, 24–25
   on Hyperloop, 62
   on importance of questions, 12
   on Internet, 17
   life as beginning entrepreneur, 17
   life as successful entrepreneur, 19, 20
   marriages of, 19, 58
   on motivation, 64
   on Orbital Sciences, 39
   on robots with artificial intelligence,
      62–63
   on solar power, 60
   on space exploration
      and colonization of Mars, 48
      and Falcon 9, 44, 45, 46
      and flying in Dragon, 44
      importance, 38
      and Mars Oasis, 36–37
      multi-planetary human life and, 47, 48
      and rockets, 41, 42–43, 47
   on viral marketing strategy, 28
   wealth of, 8, 35, 36
   on Zip2, 17, 18, 19
Musk, Errol (father), 9, 10–12, 14, 40
Musk, Justine Wilson (wife), 19–20
Musk, Kimbal (brother), 9
   on bullying of Elon in school, 10
   move to Canada by, 14
   Musk Foundation and, 63

on Zambian customs officials, 10–11
Zip2 and, 17, 18, 19
Musk, Maye (mother), 9, 10, 14
Musk, Nevada Alexander (son), 19
Musk, Tosca (sister), 8, 9, 10, 14
Musk Foundation, 63

NASA
    Commercial Orbital Transportation Services,
       43
    ISS and, 38, 40, 41, 43, 44
    Mars missions and, 37
NASDAQ, technology companies on, 30
New York Stock Exchange (NYSE), 33–35

Omidyar, Pierre, 22
online financial services
    early examples of, 22
    X.com, 22, 24, 26–27, 28
    See also PayPal
Orbital Sciences, 38–39, 40

Page, Larry, 6
Palantir, 25
Palm Pilots, 23–24
Palo Alto, California, 15–16, 16, 17
PayDirect, 28
PayPal
    creation and sale of, 8, 24
    and eBay, 26, 28, 30, 31, 33, 35
    fraud against, 32–33
    growth of, 28, 31–32, 33
    IPO, 33–35
    online financial services competition,
       28–30
    purchase of, 26–27
    working environment, 29
    X.com and, 26–27
personal digital assistants (PDAs), 23–24, 26

Queen's University (Kingston, Ontario), 14

range anxiety, 58
reading, importance of, 10, 12, 25
Ressi, Adeo, 14–15
Riley, Talulah (wife), 58
Rive, Lyndon (cousin), 57
Rive, Peter (cousin), 57
Roadster
    energy consumption, 54

first, 53–54
    pollution from, 54
    sales, 54, 55
robots with artificial intelligence, 62–63
rockets
    cost of, 37–38, 40
    reuse of, 40–41, 47
    See also Space Exploration Technologies
       (SpaceX)

September 11 terrorist attacks (2001), 33–34,
    34
Sequoia Capital, 26
SolarCity
    Businessperson of the Year Award for, 63
    charitable donations, 63
    panels for homes, 60
    Superchargers, 57–58
solar power
    electric car charging stations, 57–58
    Hyperloop, 61–62
    for ISS, 39
    Musk Foundation donations and, 63
    panels for homes, 60
solar radiation, 49
South Africa, 9, 11, 13, 13–14, 19
space exploration
    as problem important to humanity, 15, 36,
       38
    science of, 38
    See also NASA
Space Exploration Technologies (SpaceX)
    Businessperson of the Year Award for, 63
    creation of, 7, 36–38
    Dragon spacecraft, 43–44
    Falcon rockets, 40, 41, 42–43, 44–47, 46
    ISS contract, 39, 41, 44, 45
    launches for military, 42–43
    mini-satellites, 49–50
    overview of, 7–8
Stanford University, 15–16, 16
Star Wars (film), 40
stock offerings, 33–35
supercapacitors (ultra-capacitors), 15
Superchargers, 57–58

TacSat-1 (military satellite), 42
Tesla, Nikola, 51, 52
Tesla Motors
    Businessperson of the Year Award for, 63
    creation of, 51

Model S, **55**
   cost, 55–56
   cross-country trip, 57, 58
   pollution from, 7
   sales, 58
   styling and performance, 6–7, 56
Model 3 (or Model III) proposal, 58–59
P85D, 56
release of patents, 61
Roadster
   energy consumption, 54
   first, 53–54
   pollution from, 54
   sales, 54, 55
Thiel, Peter, **27**
   about, 25
   Confinity and, 24, 27
   PayPal and, 30, 32, 33, 35
   and PDAs for eBay payments, 24
Tolkien, J.R.R., 25
Tony Stark (fictional character), 64

ultra-capacitors (supercapacitors), 15
Union of Concerned Scientists, 58

Vicarious, 63
video games, first, 12
viral marketing strategy, 28

Wells Fargo, 28
Wharton School, University of Pennsylvania,
   14–15
Wilson, Justine (wife), 19–20, 58
Wired (magazine), 24
World Trade Center, 33–34, **34**

X.com
   establishment of, 26
   goal of, 24
   inspiration for, 22
   PayPal and, 26–27
   renamed, 28

Yahoo! e-commerce, 28

Zip2
   development of, 17–19
   dot-com bubble and, 20–21
   sale of, 8, 19, 21, 22

Picture Credits

About the Author

Stuart A. Kallen is the author of more than three hundred nonfiction books for children and young adults. He has written on topics ranging from the theory of relativity to the art of animation. In addition, Kallen has written award-winning children's videos and television scripts. In his spare time he is a singer/songwriter/guitarist in San Diego.